Perspectives in Christian Education

Communication - More Than Words

Philip C. Johnson, Ph. D. - Dan L. Burrell, Ed.D.

Perspectives in Christian Education
"Communication—More than Words"
© 2000 by Philip C. Johnson, Dan L. Burrell
All rights reserved

Printed in the United States of America

Packaged by WinePress Publishing, PO Box 428, Enumclaw, WA 98022. The views expressed or implied in this work do not necessarily reflect those of WinePress Publishing. Ultimate design, content, and editorial accuracy of this work are the responsibilities of the authors.

No part of this publication may be reproduced, stored in a retrieval system, or transmitted in any way by any means—electronic, mechanical, photocopy, recording, or otherwise—without the prior permission of the copyright holder, except as provided by USA copyright law.

Reproduction rights for the cover artwork, *Creation of Adam,* are granted by Tony Stone Images/Chicago Inc., copyright © 2000.

Unless otherwise indicated, all scriptures are quoted from the King James Version of the Bible.

ISBN 1-57921-313-8
Library of Congress Catalog Card Number: 00-105506

The Lancaster Baptist Church does not endorse Bible versions other than the King James Version. While we may not support every concept of this book, we feel the contents to be generally helpful for the spiritual reader.

CONTENTS

1. WHAT KIND OF COMMUNICATOR ARE YOU? 5
Philip C. Johnson

2. HOW YOU SAY IT MATTERS: COMMUNICATING
    WITH FLAIR 19
Dan L. Burrell

3. WORDS ON THE LOOSE IN THE CLASSROOM 35
Philip C. Johnson

4. COMMUNICATING WITH STYLE 47
Dan L. Burrell

5. DELIVER YOUR EXCELLENCE TO THEIR DOOR STEP 61
Philip C. Johnson

6. COMMUNICATION STARTS AT THE TOP: THE
    PASTOR'S COMMUNICATION AND A WORD FOR
    THE SCHOOL BOARD 75
Dan L. Burrell

7. COMMUNICATING THROUGH THE IRON CURTAIN:
    ADMINISTRATORS AND TEACHERS 87
Philip C. Johnson

8. GETTING THE MOST FROM YOUR METHODS: PUTTING
   POWER AND PUNCH INTO YOUR COMMUNICATION . . . 101
   Dan L. Burrell

9. LISTENING: IT'S MORE THAN JUST SITTING 113
   Philip C. Johnson

10. DEALING WITH COMMUNICATION BREAKDOWN:
    "I'M COMMUNICATING BUT NO ONE SEEMS TO
    BE PAYING ATTENTION" 125
    Dan L. Burrell

11. AWKWARD COMMUNICATION: DEALING WITH
    DIFFICULT TOPICS 137
    Philip C. Johnson

12. WHAT'S YOUR CLAIM TO FAME? COMMUNICATING
    YOUR SCHOOL'S IDENTITY 153
    Dan L. Burrell

CHAPTER ONE

WHAT KIND OF COMMUNICATOR ARE YOU?

"Communication is complex and people are complicated. Effective communication takes work, insight and practice."
—Philip C. Johnson, Ph.D

SLIPPERY WHEN TALKING!

H.B. Adams once said this about communication: "No man means all he says, and yet very few say all they mean, for words are slippery and thought is viscous." Yes, our attempts at expressing ourselves can certainly be slippery, thick, and somewhat gooey. And to complicate matters further, there is a vast variety of people out there in the world who have developed their own brand and style of communication. Yet we press forward in our attempt to understand others and to be understood. I imagine if we all knew how often we are misunderstood and how often we misunderstand others, we'd all say a whole lot less. Communication, however remains foundationally important to all relationships and for educators, it is crucial.

It certainly comes as no surprise to those who spend (or plan to spend) their professional lives communicating to others that we often miss the mark. Evidence of this surrounds us. I have always enjoyed coming across the occasional communication foible in the media over the years. Take for example, the comment made by Elizabeth Dole when she was the assistant for public liaison to President Reagan, "The President doesn't want any yes-men and yes-women around him. When he says no, we all say no." When Milwaukee Brewers Jim Gantner was trying to explain why he was late for an interview, he commented, "I must have had ambrosia." Or consider actress Brooke Shield's notable comment on smoking: "Smoking kills. If you're killed, you've just lost a very important part of your life."

Now in all fairness, it is a whole lot easier (not to mention a whole lot more fun) to point out the communication quirks of others than it is to work on improving our own communication prowess. We all, from time to time, will make statements and comments that we'd just as soon not have repeated or printed in a national magazine or newspaper. It's the nature of opening our mouths. Open it enough times and something interesting is bound to come out. But if we are going to make positive strides towards becoming more skilled communicators, we must gain some measure of control over what we say and how we say it.

It Takes More Than Wishful Thinking

My command of the Chinese language is not that good. OK, that's actually an exaggeration. In truth, my command of Chinese is not good at all. To be more exact, I don't know any Chinese words. I do like Chinese food however, especially take-out on a Friday night. But I guess that doesn't really apply here and I'm digressing from my point. What I'm trying to say is this: it would be nice if I could master

Chinese and thus become a master communicator to one-fifth of the world's population, as well as one who thoroughly understands Chinese people. Unfortunately, wishing it, or even having a healthy appreciation for the occasional egg roll, doesn't make it a reality. Effective communication requires work, and lots of it. Sadly, many approach the art of communication with the same effort they would employ to order from a take-out menu. Even communicating in one's native language doesn't guarantee effective communication. Communication is complex, and people are complicated. Effective communication takes work, insight, and practice.

Lots of People—Lots of Talk

A first step toward improving your command of communication is to attempt to understand the variety of communicators that you might encounter. It's helpful to identify the more common types of communicators as well as the innate pitfalls associated with their styles. Recognizing their qualities helps you to read between the lines more successfully. Identifying the potential pitfalls helps you to reject inappropriate communication habits from your repertoire. In the following descriptions you might recognize some people you know. You might also see yourself.

Careless Catherine. Careless Catherine says whatever pops into her head. She's often in a rush to communicate something . . . anything; therefore she doesn't always think through what she wants to say. Ann Landers says, "The trouble with talking too fast is that you might say something you haven't thought of yet." Careless Catherine is living proof of this truth. Catherine's legacy is the trail of hurt feelings she leaves behind her. If people are not hurt, they are at the very least confused by Careless Catherine's communication habits. She never means to say anything hurtful or wrong, it just sort of "pops" out. Careless Catherine often believes others are just too sensitive and that she should have the luxury of "editing" her comments *after* they come out of her mouth. She doesn't understand why her words hurt people, but she'll have plenty of time to discuss this with her last remaining friend, Ruby Regret. The underlying flaw here is a self-centered spirit more intent upon talking than interested in communicating with others. Careless Catherine needs to focus on the emotional needs of others.

Flattering Faye. Faye always makes others feel good; or at least *she* wants to feel good about making others feel good. We've all, from time to time, met someone who is a flatterer. They sweep you off your feet with their grand, sweeping, poetic compliments. You leave their presence feeling special and unique. That is, until you overhear them offering the same compliment to your roommate, or the teacher down the hall, or to your very own mother. Suddenly you realize that you are no longer that fabulous, unique work of art you had been led to believe.

The flatterer's primary concern is not with others and their feelings. Her goal is to ingratiate herself to others. It all starts innocently enough. You compliment someone's new shoes and watch their face light up. You think, "Wow! What is this new power I posses? I have the ability to make people happy, to bring a smile, to cause people to like me. Let's try it again." Before you know it, it becomes much more about you than about them. Soon you're complimenting haircuts you'd never sport, hats you'd never wear, briefcases you'd never carry, variant breathing patterns, and the occasional sneeze. And before you can say, "My, you've got the freshest breath I've ever had the pleasure of inhaling," you wake up at a FA Meeting (Flatterers Anonymous) reciting your new mantra, "I must use my compliments for good, not for my own self promotion."

The problem with flattery is that it devalues the currency of words. Flattery inflates a compliment and while it's nice to have that extra cash of confidence offered by a Flattering Faye, you'll soon find that it doesn't buy as much as it used to.

Proverbs 25:11 reminds us that, "A word fitly spoken is as apples of gold in pictures of silver." Let me emphasize the word "fitly". It has been said that an honest, appropriate compliment can last someone 30 days. An unearned or insincere compliment disappears as quickly as the hot air that produced it.

Quiet Quentin. Are you a mind reader? Quentin hopes you are. And too bad if you're not, because it's anybody's guess as to what's going on in that head of his. More than a few ladies will eventually find themselves married to a Quiet Quentin. (And some men will find themselves married to Silent Sarah.) You will recognize him as the one sitting in front of the television with the remote control cemented to his hand. Meanwhile you're trying to extract the details of the day from him.

You: "How was your day?"
Quentin: "Fine."
You: "Did you go out for lunch? What did you eat?"
Quentin: "Uh, yes . . . we had food."
You: "Well, who went with you?"
Quentin: "People from work."

11

You: "What did you talk about?"

Quentin: "Nothing really."

You: "Well, did you have that meeting with the boss? Did you get that raise? What about that transfer?"

Quentin: "Oh, yeah, I got the promotion and transfer . . . you should probably start packing. We move next Tuesday."

You get the idea. Things have to be *dragged* out of Quentin. He is no slave to the details of life. Quentin is the one who says, "I told you I loved you when I married you. If anything changes, I'll let you know." Consequently, Quiet Quentin frustrates those closest to him who desire more than a superficial relationship or who require more than the headlines at the top of the hour. Quentin needs to view communication not as a mere utilitarian tool, but as a gift he can present to someone else.

Self-Involved Seth. His friends just call him Selfish. He's so self-involved that he can't see communication from anyone else's perspective.

Chuck and Jane were newly married. Morning, noon and night Jane told her husband that she loved him pretty much to the exclusion of doing anything else. He rarely returned the verbal compliment. But every afternoon, Chuck made sure the cars were in working order, the grass was cut, the garbage was out and in his spare time he crafted everything from picnic tables to bookcases for his beloved.

It took years of frustrations and several arguments before the couple realized that they were not communicating to each other in a format the other could understand. All Chuck needed in order to know that he was loved was dinner when he came home from a long day at work and clean shirts in his closet. He didn't need to hear the words; he wanted to see actions that said, "I love you."

All Jane needed was to hear those three magic words. She could have cared less about the projects her husband was spending so much time on. She just wanted him to *tell* her he loved her. But being the intelligent couple that they were, they began communicating in the way that the other could actually "hear."

Unfortunately, not everyone catches on as quickly. Often, even when Self-Involved Seth stumbles upon the truth and actually says, "Ah, I understand now! You think *this* way and I think *that* way," he will usually just file the information away and wonder why the other person is still frustrated. He won't use the new knowledge to cause him to be a better communicator. He will simply use the information to explain or to excuse himself.

Interchangeable Irene. Irene uses words without the proper knowledge of their exchange rates. She would benefit from a good dictionary or thesaurus. She uses many words interchangeably. Words such as "like" and "love," lose their distinctions. She utters phrases like, "I'll see you around 6:00ish," not realizing the importance of giving exact information. The impact this could have on classroom homework assignments is significant!

In her mind, Interchangeable Irene usually knows what she wants, but it is rarely expressed clearly. Irene favors "indefinite" words. She is the Mistress of Misunderstanding. Sending inconsistent messages is common for her. In a classroom situation, this can be very destabilizing. She is not careful to be clear with her instructions. She does not make the important determinations between the use of pen and pencil, paper heading formats, talking and whispering, "we'll see" and "I promise."

Young people will take her at her word. They will believe what she says, regardless of the inconsistency in her communication skills. They will eventually become confused and disappointed as they begin to realize that what is said is not always what is meant. As we get older, we get more accustomed to poor and weak communication. We may improve our ability to read between the lines, but just because we get used to unacceptable communication skills, doesn't make them right. They will still produce disappointment and misunderstanding.

Passive-Aggressive Pam. Pam loves to store everything up and then just let it explode. Like squirrels storing nuts in autumn, she stores her anger and resentment away and come winter, she is stocked up 'o plenty. When you see Pam in the halls and ask her how she's doing, the answer is invariably, "Just fine!" Fine, of course until just the right moment. Her frustration builds and then she erupts all over the place and the mess is quite noticeable. Administrators recognize her as she bustles down the hall with two students he has never seen before, shrieking, "Either they go or I go!"

Instead of dealing with problems as they arise, Passive-Aggressive Pam sweeps them under the rug while her personal frustration begins its slow build. She hates confrontation and avoids it like the plague. But all of these bombs under the surface create a minefield of sorts that makes encounters with Pam unpredictable, if not dangerous.

Gossiping Gretchen. What would an educational empire be like without a school gossip? Gretchen suffers from an overload of communication skills. She loves other folks' business and loves to be "in the know." She tends to position herself near powerful or influential people. Not only does Gretchen like to know the juicy information, she *must* repeat it. Some information is just too good to keep to herself, and Gretchen is definitely a "giver." But of course, being a gossip of sterling character, she only shares it with fifty or sixty of her "closest" friends and co-workers.

Sometimes Gretchen enjoys couching her tidbits of information in the guise of a prayer request. That way she can call it "sharing" rather than gossiping. It usually goes something like this: "Oh, I just *have* to share a prayer request with you all. You all know Helen. She's just really going through a rough time right now." At this point Gretchen looks pained as if this whole subject is just too difficult to talk about; but being the trooper that she is, she forges ahead. "Don't you know, she and her husband are getting a *divorce*." (Of course the word "divorce" has to be pronounced in an exaggerated whisper to convey just how very scandalous this really is.) Gretchen pauses for dramatic effect before continuing. "And just so that we can all pray intelligently, I think you ought to know: there's another woman involved."

Eventually heads are bowed and prayers are offered, but not without everyone in the room knowing more about the situation than they need to know and wondering if the "other woman" is that blond they saw him with last week when he tried to pawn her off as his cousin.

How can we deal with gossip and the one who gossips? First, we don't need to entertain the gossip or the one sharing it. A simple and gentle rebuff is always in fashion. Secondly, we don't need to accept second-hand information. We are often far too eager to believe the worst about someone. Thirdly, if you inadvertently hear some scuttlebutt and want to find out the truth about someone you genuinely care about, go to the source, not to other friends. Finally, if you're not part of the problem or part of the solution, it's none of your business.

Blunt Bonnie. Blunt Bonnie sees life as it is. She feels no compulsion to sugar coat the facts. She tells it like she sees it. If, perchance, you have a little broccoli lingering between your teeth, don't worry—you will not be blissfully unaware for long. If your shoes do not match your belt, Bonnie will correct your fashion mistake.

Though Bonnie may often be correct in her assessments, her blunt and abrasive manner of communication doesn't exactly make her a favorite at parties. It's not her message that's always the problem; it's her delivery. Rather than slipping in the back door, pouring herself a cup of coffee and initiating an honest, yet kind conversation with her friends, she barges right through the front door, shooting first and asking questions later. Her key challenge is to choose what truly needs to be said and what needs to be overlooked. And when she does decide that something needs to be shared, she needs to employ a kinder and gentler approach.

Manipulative Marvin. Manipulative Marvin employs communication with an agenda. Marvin is difficult to identify at times. He's a master at blurring lines and confusing issues. Truth is presented as he sees it, not necessarily as it is. Rather than using communication to enhance relationships, Manipulative Marvin bends and twists language for his own benefit.

Manipulation reveals itself in a variety of forms and relationships. A child learns early in life how to manipulate Grandma and Grandpa. Usually the goal is a cookie or a later bedtime. If they deem it to be in their best interests, teenagers will do their best to pit mom against dad in the battle of dating rules and car privileges. Husbands and wives intuitively know what to say to each other to gain compliances for their wishes.

Whether it is intentional or an unconscious habit, manipulation can take on a darker, uglier visage when it is used by an adult to control others. Manipulation has the power to divide people in ministry. The best defense against a manipulator is a strong sense of truth. When in a situation where you sense you are being manipulated, do not hesitate to ask the manipulator to clarify anything he says. If necessary, request a meeting with anyone else who is involved.

Hallmarks of a Good Communicator

Whenever we tackle the subject of communication, we always need to look to the master communicator, Jesus. How blessed we are that He was clear in His message of forgiveness and salvation: "For God so loved the world that He gave His only begotten son, that whosoever believeth in Him should not perish, but have everlasting life." (John 3:16 KJV) Jesus didn't mince His words. He didn't leave His message open to misunderstanding. He didn't change His truth because His mood changed. Jesus communicated with a variety of people and in a variety of ways. He spoke to Pharisees and renowned sinners. He shared with His disciples and followers. He spoke to the women and children. He spoke through parables and sermons. When He spoke, He communicated clearly, lovingly and with integrity (though I'm sure it didn't seem so loving if you were on the business end of some of his communication!).

As we begin to change our communication habits, we need to mirror the qualities that Christ showed:
- Consistency: Giving the same message regardless of circumstances. This will produce security in students and others.
- Clarity: Saying things so that they are understood, not so that they sound impressive. This will promote understanding.
- Accuracy: Saying exactly what you mean. This will minimize misunderstandings.
- Directness: Choosing not to beat around the bush, hoping that people will "get your drift."
- Kindness: Speaking with tact. Always having the other person's best interest at heart.
- Graciousness: Choosing words that originate from a heart seasoned with grace.
- Honesty: Knowing the standard and choosing to speak the truth.
- Creativity: As long as you're talking, you might as well make it interesting!

Clear communication takes effort. It takes work and it takes understanding other people. As it has been said, "Language is the most powerful drug known to mankind." Please, use only as directed.

Chapter Two

How You Say It Matters: Communicating with Flair

"... there are few greater offenses in life than to bore someone with the Word of God."

—Dan L. Burrell, Ed.D.

Speaking for those of us who grew up in church settings, we have probably heard thousands of Bible stories in Sunday school, children's churches, and vacation Bible schools over the course of our lives. Add to those the stories we heard in school, on television, from our friends, at family reunions, around campfires, and from myriad other places, we are filled with a plethora of tales, illustrations, and stories. In my own lifetime, I have gone from chalk artists and flannel graph storyboards to high-speed, computer generated animation and Dolby surround sound. But at the core, nothing makes a good story, like a good storyteller.

One of the most effective ways to get truth across is to wrap it in a story. Everybody loves a good story. Garrison Keiller has made a fortune as "America's Storyteller" and has drawn millions of listeners to public radio who otherwise would have been watching yet another rerun of *Happy Days* or *Gilligan's Island*. The next time you are in an audience take time to notice the dynamics of the rest of the audience in relation to how they are responding to the speaker. Many times I have observed an educated speaker presenting sound material to a crowd that is mentally doing their grocery list or taking a catnap. Then, he'll pause for a second and utter a transition sentence like, "When I was a child living in the hills of Virginia . . .", and you will actually hear necks popping to attention as people tune in for the story. In most cases, once the final punch line or conclusion to the story is told, you will see many people change their posture and their attention level back to at least some degree of disconnect only listening attentively enough to pick up on the next story woven into the presentation.

Stories are effective tools for communicating truth. Perhaps the greatest storyteller of all history was the Master Teacher, Jesus. He often used illustrations from nature, parables, and object lessons to get a point across to His audience. Certainly we can learn from His example and utilize this technique for the communication of truth.

The essence of a good story can be summed up in *how* the story is told. Before we explore some keys to effective communication, I want to start with a couple of guiding principles that will help you understand the foundations of communicating through storytelling.

I begin with the premise that *there are few greater offenses in life than to bore someone with the Word of God*. I have literally grown up in church. There have been few weeks in my life when I did not attend or conduct three to five church services from Sunday school to Wednesday night Bible studies. Add to that countless revival services, school chapels, college courses and special meetings and I can imagine I have spent years under the teaching and preaching of the Word. I have listened to some teachers make the Scripture as appealing as dry toast and lukewarm water. Others however would help me notice nuances in the Scripture that I had never caught before and made me laugh at turns of phrases and subtle sarcasm woven in the Bible. I'm so thankful for those preachers, teachers and speakers who made the Bible live for me and I know it was alive to them as well.

How tragic to think that we would waste opportunities to excite thinking and provoke action while wielding the most powerful and fascinating book every authored. Yes, I realize that it is the Holy Spirit which empowers and quickens the Scripture. But that is no excuse for the preacher or teacher to handle the scripture with tedium and lethargy. It is part of our responsibility as ministers to be instruments used by the Lord to teach the truth of the Word. Romans 10:14 reminds us "How then shall they call on him in whom they have not believed? and how shall they believe in him of whom they have not heard? and how shall they hear without a preacher?" First Corinthians 1:21 goes on to state that, ". . . it pleased God by the foolishness of preaching to save them that believe." Having the privilege of teaching and preaching the Word of God is a high and holy calling.

Another principle involves getting the focus off of us. *The key to making a story live in the mind of the listener is for the storyteller to loose himself in the story.* If the presenter is worried about how he or she looks and sounds, it will become difficult to focus on the listener and the truth. Self-centeredness will always be an impediment to effective communication. It isn't about us. It's about getting the message across.

Recently, I have begun a series of daily radio broadcasts that are largely personal commentaries and opinions. I have been utilizing a vocal coach who is a professional on-air voice for a production studio. He has to constantly remind me to over-animate my voice, to smile while I am reading the script and to quit worrying about the fact that while we are recording, he is the only other person in the building. The more I think about myself (wondering privately how "cheesy" and silly I look or sound), the longer it takes us to make the broadcast sound right. And yet when I listen to my words in an animated voice versus just a regular reading, the difference is dramatic.

Effective storytellers have long forgotten or quit caring about how they look. They *become* the characters, they *live* the action, they *enjoy* the drama. In losing themselves for us, we will lose ourselves in the story and we'll walk away with a vivid impression that will remain with us, perhaps forever.

Ten Keys to Effective Story Telling

Develop a personal, animation style. No two storytellers are alike. In fact, each storyteller should be as unique as a fingerprint. You can listen to four communicators tell the same story and come away with four unique perspectives on the same event. The Holy Spirit allowed us to experience this in the Gospels as He used Matthew, Mark, Luke and John to record the life of Christ from four different angles.

To be effective, you will need to develop a unique style that allows you to be free to focus on your audience and the truth. Here are a few additional tips which will allow you to develop your own style:

Make motion a priority. Move, move, move! The human eye is uncontrollably attracted to motion. We can catch the faintest glimpse of motion from the corner of our eye and our entire body will turn to investigate it. The effective communicator will learn to make motion his or her friend. Walk around, jump and hop, wave your arms wildly, but keep the listeners attention as they wonder what you will do or where you will go next.

Use wide-sweeping gestures. Again, by using your hands and arms, you will create motion and motion keeps attention. As a general rule, your motions should be a reflection of the size crowd you are addressing. If you are speaking to one or two people, it would be ineffective, not to mention unseemly, to flail about wildly emphasizing each syllable with a dramatic gesture. Small groups allow for smaller and more subtle gestures that stay close to the body. But if you are speaking to a group of a thousand and you keep your hands in your pockets or tightly gripping the lectern with your feet frozen in place, you will soon lose the interest of the audience as their tired eyes seek solace in any winged creature flitting about the nearest light fixture which would be a welcome relief from your paralyzed presentation. Large crowds invite full-motion gestures and large dramatic motions. While it will feel exaggerated to you, from the audience's perspective, it will actually look quite normal and will be very effective. The larger the room or crowd, the greater the need for exaggerated motions. You should learn to incrementally increase your activity, motion and gestures to the size of the crowd.

Remember the limits of attention span. The mind cannot retain more than the seat can endure. Due to the increase in visual stimulation and choices and the addiction many in our culture have to sitcoms and sound bites, our attention span is probably being reduced each day. The wise communicator takes this into account and compensates by varying his presentation, reducing its length and providing breaks and variations throughout the lesson.

A general rule for attention span is approximately one minute per year of age. Therefore, a kindergartner who sits still and listens for more than five minutes is a wonder child and should be promptly rewarded with candy corn and M & M's® which will adequately restore the kid to an appropriate attention span deficit. Junior high kids can't be expected to "hang in there" for more than twelve to fourteen minutes. Most people "top out" at around twenty to twenty-five minutes with a few rare people hanging in there longer, but only if they are listening to an exceptional speaker.

Therefore, the wise kindergarten teacher breaks her class into segments that do not exceed five minutes. By giving a four-minute story and then a two-minute exercise which is followed by a four-minute drill and reinforced with a three-minute song before concluding with a two-minute review, a fifteen-minute lesson becomes more productive, discipline problems are reduced, and information is retained without some poor five-year old exploding while trying to sit through the full lesson without a break.

Use your voice effectively. The individual who views his or her voice as an instrument makes oral communication effective. It is essential to acknowledge the effective tool that exists in each of us and to find ways of using it to our advantage and for the good of our students. There are four aspects of effective voice usage.

Pitch. Your pitch has to do with the level or qualities of your voice and how you construct your sentences using those qualities. You will vary your pitch in normal conversation depending on the type of sentence you are speaking.

Usually, you will end an interrogative sentence with an upward pitch as you conclude the question. Read this question out loud so you can hear your own voice utilize pitch: "Will you be having dessert after your meal?" Notice how you ended your sentence by raising the pitch of your voice. Now change the same sentence into a declarative sentence and notice your pitch. "You will be having dessert after your meal." Notice that you didn't vary your pitch a great deal. You just issued a statement. Finally, make the sentence imperative as if you were giving an order. "You will be having dessert after your meal!" Did you hear and feel the pitch and intensity change? These are examples of "pitch."

This is important because pitch allows you to add expression and emotion to what you are saying. In addition, you should remember to exaggerate the pitch and other vocal styling incrementally according to the size of the crowd.

Speed. The speed with which you speak adds drama, intensity and excitement to your dialogue. By slowing your speech dramatically, you can cause people to anticipate and strain for the next word that gives you their undivided attention. Such listening is wearisome, so there must be limit to the length of utilizing such a method, but it is very effective. On the other hand, by accelerating your speech, suddenly or incrementally, you can reawaken the listener, create a sense of impending action, dramatize the action of the story with drama and tension or even create the illusion of rapid passage of time. An instrument always played with the same tempo eventually becomes monotonous. We enjoy a variety of speeds in music and your audience will enjoy the same variations with your voice.

Volume. Louder is not always better nor is silence always golden. But the range between shouting and whispering contains many opportunities to capture and recapture your audience's attention. As you lower your voice to nearly a whisper, the listeners will find themselves straining to catch the words and anticipating your next phrase. They will ease forward in their seats, become very silent themselves and will listen intensely so as not to miss a single syllable. But this is only good for a limited period of time. Eventually, the listener would decide this is too much work and begin thinking about something else. Conversely, volume can be used to catch the listener off guard and surprise him with drama or punctuation. Moving from a slow-paced whisper to a sudden shout and rapid-fire description is the verbal equivalent of the lioness who is creeping up on her prey and with a sudden leap and a roar springs into action and chases it across the prairie before capturing it in her jaws. By utilizing speed and volume, you have an extremely effective combination to create interest and add drama.

Tone. I remember well how my mother would tell me the story of "Goldilocks and the Three Bears." My favorite parts were when she assumed the voice of each of the three bears. "Daddy Bear" had a big growling voice that was as bass as my tiny mother could make it. "Momma Bear" used soothing tones not unlike those my mother usually used. "Baby Bear" spoke in a high-pitched, squeaky tone normally reserved for dog whistles and mosquitoes. By using tone effectively, she was able to assume the role of each bear in a unique and delightful way. Whether you are playing Goliath, reading Shakespeare, describing a waterfall, or role-playing Jonathon Edwards, your tone will be a tremendous asset to pointing the student to your objective and the message.

Use visual illustrations. The mind and attention are drawn to motion and images. One of the primary goals of the effective communicator is to draw mental pictures for the listener. Whether in writing or in speaking, descriptive communication will capture the attention of the reader or listener and will give you the opportunity to teach your objective.

Capture the imagination with vivid descriptions. I can say "I had a peach for breakfast," or I can say, "This morning, I found one perfect peach nestled in a basket of assorted fruit on my kitchen counter. The sun coming through the window seemed to invite me to this particular orb. It had a deep hue of crimson beneath its gentle fuzz. As the dappled light announced its ripeness, I felt just the right 'give' as I picked it up. Biting into its velvety skin, I sensed the splash of juice erupt from its felt and race down my arm." I'll stop here in my imagery so I can run to the fruit stand. Now which description caused you the more vivid mental image? Use all the senses you possibly can to capture the imagination.

Utilize real-life objects. You don't have to have sophisticated magic tricks or hard-to-repeat chemical reactions to have an object lesson. Something as simple as a rock, a picture, a magazine, or an instrument will draw the attention of the listener and when you have the attention, you are more likely to be able to communicate your point.

Insert visual images. Again, using pictures and images will give you control over the attention, focus, and alertness of your audience. Motion always attracts attention and by inserting visual images periodically, you will be able to recapture the listener's attention. Keep in mind that we all think more rapidly than we are able to speak. Therefore, the speaker must be aware that the mind of his or her listeners is probably racing ahead of the words much of the time. By inserting visual images, you will throw a temporary diversion or hurdle in the mind of audience members which gives you time to catch up. Here are a few methods of "insertion."

Use overhead projectors. Of course, this is the staple tool of many classroom teachers. It allows you to face the audience. Never turning your back on a group of students may be one of the wisest teaching tactics you'll ever use. Today's overhead projectors allow you to write on film, prepare transparencies in advance, and even use a special attachment that will project your computer screen onto the wall. More cumbersome, but still effective is the opaque projector that will give you the opportunity to project non-transparent items like photos and maps onto the wall.

Use *Powerpoint®* presentations. Microsoft has a terrific program called *Powerpoint®,* which produces graphics that are projectable via a video imager or onto a television monitor. You can utilize color, sound, animation, video and audio clips, artwork, websites and many other attention-gathering formats in a *Powerpoint®* presentation. The program is contained in most office suites or software bundles on today's computers or you can purchase it individually. There are many technology toys which will enhance your presentation. To master *Powerpoint®*, you might want to take a class or get a text such as *Powerpoint for Dummies* to help you gain access to all of its applications.

Use video. The use of VHS and DVD formats for visual reinforcement is a great option. It is not, however, a substitute for teaching. Nor is it an appropriate utilization of technology for crowd control (for example, putting in a *Veggie Tales®* video so the teacher can count the lunch money). But taking clips or even occasionally viewing the entire presentation of a drama or play is acceptable. Another use of a video camera is through the use of projection devises, which allow a camera to project a close-up image onto a screen so that more people can see the detail. This is particularly effective when used in science labs. Performing a "live" dissection and projecting it so that all the students can see it is a great way to keep the students alert while you teach.

Use flashcards, flannelgraph, etc. Of course, we can't neglect the old staples of flashcards, flannelgraph and other less sophisticated visuals. These are still very effective for younger children and occasional use elsewhere.

Make it memorable. The use of trivia, illustrations, and surprising information is essential in the presentation of material that you want others to recall later. The human mind will usually recall information that is unique, unusual, surprising or even bizarre. I fill my library with books of trivia and keep files of unusual statistics, anecdotes, and information for the purpose of spicing up my lessons, sermons, and lectures. Quotations and epigrams are additional tools for etching key principles into the mind of the reader. If you see the listener look up and lean forward or pick up a pen and jot something down, you've hit the mark!

Weave your lesson throughout the story. I have spoken in a hundred chapel services for elementary and secondary students and watched them "shut down" when they realized I was making my final point in my message. Bibles close, pencils are put away and students reach for book bags. If I save my key point for the last thirty seconds of the lesson, I might as well forget it. They are already mentally preparing for math class by that time. Don't save your lesson objective for the end. Instead, use this three-step strategy.

- Preview. *Tell them what you will tell them in your lesson.*

- Present. *Tell them the lesson and remind them of the point.*
- Review. *Tell them what you told them as you conclude the lesson.*

Exaggerate motion and details. Webster defines the term *exaggerate* as "to give an elaborate account of." It may feel odd to move around extensively or to use wide, sweeping gestures, but it will draw your listeners to you and your message. It may seem wordy and even awkward to be very descriptive or detailed, but it will often paint the picture in the mind of your audience that will last beyond the length of your lecture. Here are some areas for "elaboration":

Colors. You can make it red or you can make it a deep, pulsating crimson.

Sounds. It can be a bang or you can call it a low, grumbling roar that crescendoed into a horrific explosion.

Atmosphere. It can be a basement or you could describe it as a damp and dank cellar filled with cobwebs and the smell of mustiness usually reserved for tombs or crypts.

Smells. It can be smelly or you can wrinkle noses by describing it as an acrid and pungent odor that caused you to gasp from its stench.

Suggested Dialogue. It is fun to use (clearly-stated) suggested dialogue which creates mental images and causes the listener to relate. *Then little David looked across the rocky valley and put his hands on hips and shouted, "Hey Goliath! I hope you are ready to die today because with God's help, I'm going to take you down!"*

Illustrate every point you want them to remember. Illustrations are key to causing the audience to remember your topic and objectives. We love stories and trivia. Take the time before your lesson to look for stories, quote, fun-facts, illustrations, and anecdotes that recapture the attention of the listener and which will "mark" the objective in their mind through the illustration.

Insist on having the attention of the audience. If the audience isn't listening or can't hear you, they won't be impacted by your lesson. Some mistakenly feel that simply leaking out a loud and prolonged *ssssshhhhhh* will cause everyone to fall into silence and begin listening. In fact, using that method may be the least-effective way of gaining or regaining attention. In the end, they will ignore you and you sound silly—as if you've sprung a sudden leak. Here are a few specific ideas:

"1-2-3 Zip". Good for smaller students, act like you are zipping your lip and then remain silent until everyone is quiet.

Lower your voice. By getting gradually quieter and softer in volume and tone, the students will lower their own voices so that they can hear you.

"Watch This!" By pointing and/or snapping the fingers while saying "Watch This!" you can often redirect focus and attention.

Finger on the lips. This can be a signal that when everyone is silent, we will continue.

Established signal. Train your class that when a bell is rung, a light is flickered, a chime is sounded, or whatever your preferred signal may be, that all unnecessary noise and movement is to cease.

Use first names. With older students, sometimes utilizing the name of an inattentive student very casually into your sentences will cause them to pay attention and be more alert.

Involve the audience. Use interactive drills, games, and participation strategies to invite the listeners into the story on a personal level. Here are a few techniques for this method:

Role Play. You be Goliath and let one of your smaller students be David. Everyone will be watching and you'll get your point across.

Assistant. Have someone stand next to you and hand you items, put things on the board, help with the experiment. Hoping that they'll be called on to help, you'll have the riveted attention of the rest of the class.

Response. Use games and questions to get class response in unison and out-loud for certain key points or objectives.

There is no way that the subject of communicating with flair has been exhausted in this chapter, but I hope it gives you some starting points that will inspire you to liven up your classes and capture the attention of your students. Communicating with flair should be a hallmark of every effective teacher!

Chapter Three

Words on the Loose in the Classroom

*"Use your words as a surgeon would use a knife . . .
with exact precision, for an exact purpose."*
—Philip C. Johnson, Ph.D.

My wife and I met in college. She is a native Korean, and English is definitely her second language. Needless to say, we are no strangers to communication issues, some of which have teetered on the brink of becoming a major international incident. While I was driving everyone home from school one day, my wife decided that this would be an ideal time to quiz my youngest son, Sam, over his spelling words. It seemed to be a good idea . . . mother helping son . . . education being advanced. What harm could come of this familial tutelage?

Things began just fine. Words were stated; words were spelled. I sat a little taller in the driver's seat as my then second-grade son mastered words like *animal, house* and *candle*. I began daydreaming about future spelling bees, national championships and the like when a pot hole brought me back to the little bee going on in my car.

My wife called out the word, "son." Sam dutifully replied, "s-o-n." Moving on to the next word on the list, my wife called out, "again." And Sam repeated himself, "s-o-n." "*Again!*" repeated my wife, a little more clearly this time.

And Sam replied just as clearly, "s-o-n." "**Again**," barked my wife. "S-o-n," replied Sam, with slightly less confidence.

By this time, my wife thought that Sam was just being defiant, so she called out even more loudly, "*AGAIN!*" Meanwhile, Sam was convinced that his otherwise healthy mother had suddenly gone deaf. He very loudly and clearly spelled out the word yet one more time, "**S-O-N!**"

Amazingly, this pattern continued without either of them realizing what was going on. My wife got louder and louder while Sam continued to offer the same answer, each time a little more tearfully. Sam had no clue that his mother was on a completely different spelling word, and my wife could not understand how Sam could have suddenly become such a poor speller.

Somewhere around the ninth exchange of "again" followed by "s-o-n", my older son, much more aware of homophones, decided to help out. He leaned over to the very frustrated, quivering-voiced Sam, and said, "Maybe she's looking for 's-u-n.'"

Meanwhile, I'm banging my head repeatedly against the steering wheel mentally calculating the future therapy bills.

Talking is basic to conveying information. But just because we're talking doesn't necessarily mean that we're being understood. And if we're not being understood, then we're not communicating. If communicating in a clear, accurate, and effective fashion is important for all of us who walk upright and breathe, then it is simply *crucial* for those of us who are communicating to students in the classroom. As Christian educators, we need to sense the importance of the information that we share with our students. We are sharing more than just mere facts and figures; we are sharing life-changing truths that will impact eternity. Improving communication skills in the classroom requires the examination of several facets regarding this topic.

Words Have Power

They're just words, you know. Nothing more than an assortment of consonants strung together with the appropriate number of vowels inserted. Put a few of those words together and you're likely to get a phrase, or if you're highly intelligent, you'll find yourself with a full-blown sentence on your hands, just moments away from a paragraph and perhaps that little romantic novel you've always dreamed of writing. Words may not seem to be much when we think of them in that context, but if you've ever heard them come out of someone's mouth, you know that there is so much more to this whole *words brouhaha* thing we've been hearing so much about.

Words have the ability to conjure up very strong emotional responses. Just think of words like "mother," "prison," "summer school," and "bonus check." Each of these words causes an emotional response ranging from warm feelings of love and anticipation to dread or fear. Words have power; there's no doubt about it. Words also have the ability to build students up or to tear them down; to exalt or to devastate. And if you've been a teacher for more than a day, you know how quickly this can happen.

As an educator in the classroom, you have at your disposal an impressive arsenal of words. And to give you even more leverage, you're the one in charge, you're older than your students, you possess a more diverse vocabulary, and you're probably just plain bigger than your charges. Now, repeat after me, "I must use my powers for good, not for evil . . . I must use my powers for good, not for evil . . ."

The fact is, words are the primary tools of our trade. They can be used or misused. We can and will change the lives of the students in our classes based on what comes out of our mouths. We have reason to give special attention to our words and to how we intend to use them.

In our current culture that worships comfort, many of us trade accuracy of speech for convenience. Often our words are not crafted as carefully as they might be, thus sometimes wounding and confusing those around us. Because we're working with impressionable young minds, it becomes crucial that we take care how we phrase things. It's important to know how students might take what we say. Here are some examples:

Teacher says: "How dumb can you get?"

Students hear: "I'm not very smart, so why should I try?"

Teacher says: "You're the messiest group of students I know."

Students hear: "I'll never be neat enough for this teacher."

Teacher says: "I'm just wasting my breath on this class."

Students hear: "My teacher likes to lecture. It makes him/her feel better and like s/he's in control."

Teacher says: "Can't you do anything right?"

Students hear: "Don't try anything new."

Teacher says: "Knock it off, class clown."

Students hear: "Try not to get caught next time."

This kind of careless communication might get your initial point across and it will certainly get some sort of reaction from your class, but it also can wound the spirit of the student and limit that child's future. Sometimes I believe that vocabularies should come with a warning label: "May cause emotional harm, please use with care. Do not exceed recommended dosage and never, ever use while angry."

Say What You Mean!

When it comes to most communication, there are usually two types of problems that occur: no communication and unclear communication.

No communication is fairly self-explanatory. It occurs when someone just keeps his mouth shut. No information is conveyed. No thoughts are shared. No great debates occur. No secret loves are revealed. No learning takes place. You get the idea.

In the case of unclear communication, however, there is plenty said, but no one is really sure as to what is meant. Predictably, the result is misunderstanding. And of course, misunderstanding begets confusion and confusion leads to frustration and frustration promotes the erection of emotional walls. Here are some ideas for improving communicative clarity in the classroom:

Don't assume students already know. Yes, even though you told them yesterday, and the day before that, they simply don't remember. Yes, we can enter into a huge debate about responsibility and listening skills and somewhere along the line we'll end up blaming these non-listening students for the national debt. But for now, trust me. If you want to be clearer in the classroom, don't assume that students already know it or have already heard it. They're not mind readers, and they often can't remember what you may have said yesterday, let alone last month.

When giving directions for assignments or projects, remember the following:
- All directions/instructions should be in writing.
- Include all expectations.
- Include all dates/deadlines.
- List all tools that will be necessary to complete the assignments/project.
- Go over the written instructions orally.
- Tattoo the instructions to their foreheads.

Ask students if they have any questions. You always want to provide an opportunity for clarification. And some students will ask the very same question a shy student would never ask.

Ask the students questions to make sure they understand fully. Most teachers have had the experience of sharing information and instructions with a class, asking if there are any questions and much to their delight, not a hand goes up. Obviously we assume that we are master communicators, and we begin to mentally clear room on our mantle for the inevitable teacher-of-the-year trophy. Then when it comes time for that project or assignment to be turned in, it becomes tragically clear that somewhere, somehow, something went wrong.

Some students are so lost and so unsure of what to do, they can't even formulate an intelligent question. Therefore, they just sit there, staring at you. You, not being sure if this is the stare of enlightenment, the stare of the empty-headed, or the stare of empty stomachs, might assume that students are clear on the assignment when what they really might need is a tuna sandwich. Assume that their minds are in the lunchroom and ask them questions to help you know if they have understood what you have presented.

Review and remind. Part of being a good communicator is understanding the human condition and weakness. Even great oral communicators understand that more of their message will be heard and retained through review and repetition.

BODY LANGUAGE AND TONE

Not everything that is communicated necessarily comes from the mouth. Our bodies can convey a lot of information as well. Many people do not realize it, but they often communicate volumes to their students before they even begin teaching the lesson.

Sitting at the desk while teaching communicates passiveness. It conveys that you're not really interested in what you're teaching; that you're tired; that the students may not be important enough for you to bother standing to your feet.

Walking around the classroom communicates control and presence. It shows that you probably didn't stay up until 2:00 a.m. and that you're prepared to teach. It also shows that you didn't just fall off the turnip truck, but that you understand that there may be all kinds of interesting things going on in the back of the classroom—stuff you wouldn't dream of missing.

Standing behind the lectern communicates that you may not know your material. There you are, held hostage by your text book . . . in bondage to the printed page. It communicates a very sad indirect message to your students.

Freedom from the lectern implies confidence. It confirms to your students that you are a master of the material; that information and insights flow from your educated soul. OK, they may not say it exactly like that, but believe me, it will have a more positive effect than standing behind your lectern.

Hand motions and voice tone can imply enthusiasm, excitement or the lack thereof. You can't fake enthusiasm. Students know whether or not you love teaching and whether or not you love them. So first, fix any wrong attitudes and then communicate your joy through your hands and voice.

A breath mint can imply respect. Trust me . . . they notice.

A touch on the shoulder or a smile can communicate warmth and encouragement. Never underestimate the importance of appropriate human contact. Many students, when they view the hand of God, will reflect back on that teacher—that earthly representation of God on earth—who lovingly reached out and took their dirty, sometimes grubby hand in an act of love and acceptance.

THE WAY YOU TEACH COMMUNICATES A LOT

A teacher's individual style indirectly contributes much in the way of effective communication in the classroom. The most carefully thought out words, from the purest of hearts, will do little to affect the lives of others if they are presented in such a way as to lure students into a coma. Even effective communicators need to remind themselves of the tools of classroom teaching style.

Use variety. A US Navy study revealed that listeners lose concentration after about 18 minutes into a lecture or speech. OK, so they weren't studying kindergarteners . . . or 5th graders . . . or 11th graders. OK, so maybe they weren't studying anyone we have ever personally met, but still, the point is people have a tendency to let their minds wander. So variety is a good thing. Teach for 10 or 12 minutes then use a game, tell a story, or view part of a video. Ask some questions, have a discussion, or use an effective illustration.

Use stories. Stories, illustrations, or anecdotes are wonderful classroom tools. Boys, not often known for their ability to express their emotions, are especially susceptible to the power of the well told story. Many boys and men are moved to make spiritual decisions based on stories that they hear.

Be enthusiastic. It's simply contagious. If you're excited, then your students will be excited.

Be prepared. Preparation shows that you've put thought into what you're going to teach. It affects the flow of the lesson as well.

Use vivid language. Try to be a little creative. Instead of saying that the desert was "hot," say that it was "torrid." Your trip to Alaska exposed you to "frigid," not "cold" temperatures. Don't tell students that people "walk"; tell them they "saunter," "stroll," or "gallop." Don't request a "little" cream in your coffee, but a "whisper of cream," or perhaps nothing more than a "murmur of cream."

Make your lesson practical. Sadly, today's students are more cynical than ever. They simply do not accept education at face value. Effective classroom communicators know that they need to make what they teach relevant to students. If students can't see for themselves how vital your class is, make it your personal mission to lead them to the point of understanding how life changing it is to drink from the well of your knowledge.

Be concise. People don't remember all we say anyway. Enough said.

Use humor. A little humor can go a long way in your classroom. It can lighten a tense moment. It can provide a warm memory of a shared laugh. It can cause students to remember an important fact or principle forever.

Remember, if you're not keeping students' attention, then you're not communicating effectively. There is much more to communication than just standing in front of a classroom with students and talking.

What You Don't Say

Neglect in communication is as troublesome as inaccurate and ineffective communication. The only thing that is equally as troubling as misunderstanding what someone actually says, is trying to guess what someone is thinking but never says. A perfect illustration of this is the story of an old farmer who sat on his porch one day pondering the good qualities of the wife who had shared the last forty-two years of her life with him. As he was thinking of her faithfulness, love and devotion, he leaned over to her and said, "Martha, you have meant so much to me over these last forty-two years, sometimes I can hardly keep from telling you."

How often we mirror the same action, sharing all that we're unhappy about but forgetting to share the positive. The adage, "no news is good new," never applies to interpersonal communication. (It does apply in cases of war and hints of visits from your mother-in-law, but that's another story.) While we are often quick to communicate the negative, for some reason, we let many opportunities to communicate positive things slip by. The teacher dedicated to being a better communicator knows that it is crucial to communicate positive things to and about students as often as possible. Students desperately want to hear not only good things from you, but they also want an honest appraisal of their academic progress.

THE ART OF WORDS

As a final challenge to communicators in the classroom, let me remind you that we should view our words as colors chosen carefully from a palette. Words have meaning, specific meanings. Words also pack emotion and contain nuance. Synonyms are fun, but there's nothing like the satisfaction of choosing exactly the right word for the right situation. Use the words you mean to use. Use your words as a surgeon would use a knife . . . with exact precision, for an exact purpose. And as with a doctor, choosing to use a sharp and precise scalpel will get the job done a lot faster, and with a lot less pain than say, using a butter knife.

Chapter Four

Communicating with Style

"Educators must awaken to the reality that communication is changing and in most of our cases has not just overtaken us, but left us in its exploding wake."

—Dan L. Burrell, Ed.D.

We live in an age that is literally exploding with communication. We are bombarded with a non-stop blast of messages, signals, impressions and perspectives virtually every waking moment. The marvels of technology have not only accelerated the introduction of new and better forms of communication, but have raised our expectations as we have grown accustomed to variety, convenience, excellence, and innovation. And for better or worse, there is no sign that this age of communication will be abating for quite some time.

In virtually every mall, pop singers ring our ears and catch our attention from a score of video monitors who beam every gyration and syllable to us in technicolor and surround sound. As we tool down the corridor, one of two hundred available tones compiled into scores of ditties and songs alert us to an incoming call from our cellular phone which may transmit the voice of a friend or loved one via digital or analog technology. Once we arrive at home, we collapse on our couch and reach for the television remote where we mindlessly thumb our way through as many as one hundred twenty different channels, networks, and services. Our home entertainment add-on package allows us to hear the advertising, music, and dialogue from every direction and even experience the rumble of deep-bass explosions and propulsions. If they aren't beaming what we want at the moment to us, we can run down to one of the tens of thousands of video stores in our country and chose between a VHS or DVD format of virtually every movie ever created (unless we want to call our cable service operator and have our selection beamed directly to us). Or rather than expend all that energy, we move over to our computer work station and with the touch of a key or two, we can access the Internet and the World-Wide Web via phone modem, T1 cable, satellite uplink, or the new DTS service we can obtain through our local phone company. Within seconds, we can download books onto our handheld computers, visit websites of places in every corner of the world, compete with people we will never meet in one of a thousand different games, chat with strangers in virtual rooms, search for information and data from the world's largest universities, libraries, and institutions, listen to live radio or watch live video from scores of cities, transmit photos, audio, or video images back and forth to our family across the country, send an email to two or a hundred people simultaneously, register for a service, purchase an item, take a college course for credit, look for a new job, find an old friend, sell the junk in your garage or buy the junk from someone else's, publish your own site, or take part in myriad other activities on this newest hub of information and communication.

Within this environment, all over the country, a dear and sincere schoolteacher will walk down the corridor of her school building, leaving a trail of papers and stick'em notes as she wrestles with an armload of textbooks and newly copied assignment papers. Plopping them onto the desk, the teacher looks out across a roomful of teenagers and shifts gears to begin communicating the educational objectives which she has meticulously recorded with number two pencil in her lesson plan book. She reaches into her desk drawer and pulls out a small cardboard box. With a few fumbling motions, she opens the top and shakes and rolls the box looking for the one remaining piece of classroom chalk that has not yet been broken. Grasping the powdery stick, she makes her way over to a board worn with age, but still clinging to a coat of green or black paint and begins writing the rules, salient points, and homework assignments for her class that day. Mid-way through her notations, she notices that the room is oddly silent except for the occasional spine-tingling screech of chalk on board. Finding the silence odd, if not eerie, she turns to inspect her class. It is then that she realizes that they have collectively disconnected through sleep, daydreaming, or sheer boredom and are oblivious to what she is trying to teach.

Educators must awaken to the reality that communication is changing and in most of our cases has not just overtaken us, but left us in its exploding wake. Our students are more sophisticated, articulate, educated, and demanding in their expectations and demands for communication than any generation that has ever existed. We compete with Hollywood, Nintendo®, and the internet for our students attention and often, we don't put up much of a fight. For the educator to be as effective as possible, he or she will have to grow knowledgeable of the styles, types and methods of communication, gain working skills on how it can be applied in the classroom, and give every effort to using these new and exciting applications and innovations in such a way that students learn the truth of Scripture and the skills they will need for living.

Ultimately, there are many ways in which we can chose to communicate. How we communicate is often a matter of style. One's communication style is usually a mix of methods and approaches for getting our point across. It will vary by individual, by audience, by venue, and by design. It is in our development of a communication style that we may hold the key to our level of success as a communicator and as a teacher.

Too often, teachers take an army's cook approach to teaching. The greasy-aproned cook in the company messhall can slop a spoonful of runny eggs onto a piece of burnt toast that's garnished with some straight-out-of-the-can fruit cocktail and anticipate that the newly-shorn recruit has two options and two options only. He can eat or he can be hungry. It doesn't much matter to the cook.

The teacher who is committed to communication takes a different tact. He understands that students will rarely retain those things that he or she considers boring, irrelevant, or inconsequential. They may briefly hold onto enough data to regurgitate the correct answers onto a multiple-choice test for a passing grade, but ultimately it makes no lasting impact. But a student who gets excited and interested in the truth, principle, or method being taught will not see the lesson as an exercise or an end, but as the beginning of a process that takes root in the classroom, blossoms outside of the school, and bears fruit throughout a lifetime. It is toward that end that teachers should be striving to be communicators with style and excellence. Otherwise, our students will simply leave our information "mess hall" for someplace more appealing.

Methods of Communication

It is impossible to list every method of communication that is in use or available today. However, it is important to recognize the categories in which those methods incubate. Methods are the tools we use to gain entrance to our students minds for the purpose of provoking thought and action. It is through the senses that we exploit those portals and transfer our information.

Sound. From the use of our voices to the power of music, from the trill of a bird to the rush of a windstorm, from the void of silence to the exhaustion of traffic noise, sound has an impact on us. No other weapon in the arsenal of the teacher is more effective in communication than the use of sound, and the key to sound will always be the human voice.

Sight. Our culture has grown increasingly more sensitive to visual images as our technology has improved. One hundred years ago, moving pictures were a novelty, color photographs unheard of and visual imagery was usually live and in person. Shelves were lined with non-descript books filled with pages of black and white information. Today, colors leap at us from every angle, motion is a constant, three-D images are no longer unique, and everywhere we look, someone is trying to catch our attention using sight.

Touch. Tactile communication will always be uniquely human and divinely appointed. The blind learned the power of touch as a tool for learning as they expanded their mind with sensitive fingertips scrolling over pages of bumps and dots. For all of us, the sensation of feeling the down of a chick, the slimy scaliness of a reptile, or the reassuring pressure of a teacher's hand on our shoulder as she whispers "I like the way you made those letters" is an important part of learning and reinforcement.

Taste. A science teacher can describe the locations of the various types of taste buds on a human tongue and the students may indeed remember it for a quiz or test. But the teacher who brings a slice of lemon, a packet of salt, a pinch of sugar or a leaf from a bitter herb for his students to experience the locations personally will be the teacher longer remembered and will etch the reality onto their students far more effectively.

Smell. Some scientists have concluded that the most powerful sense may ultimately be the sense of smell. A smell can seduce or repulse. It can cause one to experience a *déjà vu* sensation that transmits them to an earlier time in their life with a mere whiff of pumpkin pie, the odor of a freshly cut Christmas tree, or the essence of a lilac blossom.

The effective teacher will learn to use every available sensory portal as they communicate the facts, figures, and truths to their students. Whether using sticks and apples to teach math, a tape of British actors reading Shakespeare in literature class, a disemboweled fetal pig in anatomy, a blindfolded "taste test" exercise in a life development course, or a few acrid chemical reactions in chemistry, we can communicate with greater style and effectiveness when we go beyond mere words and stimulate the senses.

Nonverbal Communication

Much of our communication will involve the use of words and truly, words are the bricks and mortar of our communication. It is possible, but difficult to communicate information without them. But utilizing nonverbal forms of communication will clarify, magnify, and intensify the core of what we hope to communicate. There are various nonverbal means of communication.

Silence. Silence can be extremely uncomfortable. Many of our students will state their "need" for noise. They do their homework with a stereo or television on. They like lots of laughter around them. Racket fills their lives. It is possible to emphasize a point with a long pause or even regain attention by falling totally mute for sixty seconds. In the long run, we would be spiritually healthier if we would listen more and appreciate silence. Psalm 46:10 reminds us to "Be still, and know that I am God: I will be exalted among the heathen, I will be exalted in the earth."

Sound. Teachers have used "sound" to gain or regain attention for as long as there have been students. Snapping fingers, clapping hands, banging books, or my personal favorite—the dreaded *ssssshhhhhhh* (always the sound of a teacher who has already lost control, doesn't really know how to regain it, and has resorted to making a sound like she has sprung a leak which is invariably ignored by those for which it was attended making her *look* foolish, as well as sound foolish.)

Demeanor. A teacher who slouches into class wearing an open-collared shirt, jeans, and tennis shoes communicates something about the class, teacher, and expectations which is probably the total opposite of what is communicated by the teacher who walks in briskly, moves confidently, dresses professionally, and speaks authoritatively. They may actually *say* the same things, but *how* they present it will make all the difference as to whether or not it is caught by the students.

Attitude. The communicator who believes in what she is saying will always be more effective than the person who is just providing lip-service. The teacher who eats, breathes, and drinks grammar and composition will approach teaching a course of senior level language arts with a totally different frame-of-mind and attitude than she will if asked to teach a section of seventh grade math. She may communicate to both groups of students, but we all know that the better her attitude, the better the communication. This is why forcing teachers to take classes out of field often backfires for the student. If you aren't excited about the topic, it is hard to communicate it effectively.

Posture. Sometimes called "bearing" or "presence," a communicator's posture can either communicate command, confidence and control or it can express disinterest, discouragement and disenchantment. The professional communicator is mindful of the details of presentation and posture and sees them as essentials not trifles. Michelangelo is often quoted as having said, "Trifles make perfection and perfection is no trifle."

Space prevents us from exploring every single facet of non-verbal communication, but the list would include volume, diction, preparation, eye contact, gestures, inflections, intensity, motion, and integrity.

Ten Keys to Effective Communication

The teacher must have a good grasp of the information to be taught. As fundamental as this may seem, many teachers, preachers, and communicators will try to bluff their way through material they've never truly learned for themselves. Some pull it off to some extent through sheer showmanship and bravado, but in the end, they weaken the process and do a disservice to the listener.

Use a variety of methods. Don't be a slave to a single type or style of communication. Aren't you glad that there is more art than just landscapes? Wouldn't it be boring if the only type of theatre we could enjoy was reader's theatre? How boring life would be if there was only one item on every menu! You can vary volume, speed, visuals, intensity, costumes, format, timing, methods, and a hundred other facets of communication to keep your information exciting, your application relevant and your audience alert.

Stretch your vocabulary. The teacher should always be challenging the student audience. If you never use a new word, teach a new definition, or speak slightly above or ahead of them, they will soon come to the conclusion that they probably know about as much as you do. Avoid overwhelming them with ridiculously obscure words, but paint vivid and descriptive pictures that will stimulate and tantalize their cogitation.

Believe in it and show it. It is hard to feign interest over a prolonged period of time. If you don't believe in what you are teaching, it will be difficult for you to inspire your students to acknowledge or embrace the truth that may be contained in your message. Belief stirs passion and intensity in the communicator. It promotes depth and substance. If you are just playing the role of communicator without actually buying into what you are teaching, then you should probably consider a more honest way of earning a living.

Enthusiasm is contagious. We've all seen Hollywood's depiction in recent years of the boring, monotone and nasal science teacher who turns everything from chemistry to sex education into a coma-inducing drone-fest. In fact, some of us actually had him in the eleventh grade. Then there's the energetic and enthusiastic teacher who acts like she couldn't sleep last night because she was so excited about teaching today's lesson. This individual could sell ice-cubes to Eskimos and you soon discovered that conjugating a verb was indeed thrilling. The difference is communication energized by enthusiasm. Don't lose it!

Solicit feedback and gauge responses. You can measure your own effectiveness by soliciting feedback from your audience. No, you don't have to provide handy little "Class Evaluation Forms" after every class period. You can gain insight into how your communication style is working by being alert. Boring teachers have discipline problems. Dull lectures put people to sleep. You must admit that you have lost students who are doodling or are reading from another book in their lap while you are teaching. The alert teacher doesn't ignore these signals. By alert observation, asking questions, measuring class participation, and utilizing other feedback tools, you can tell if the message is arriving where it is intended to be delivered.

Make immediate adjustments when necessary. Even the best communicator will lose his audience from time to time. Classes go through moods and seasons. Every teacher knows that teaching the week before Christmas is always challenging. Students are far more wiggly the day after Halloween or Valentine's Day when the sugar-buzz is still in play. Kids after lunch would often like to take a nap. When you see that you are losing or have lost your audience, then take action! Have them stand, ask questions, tell a story, ask for an illustration, play a board game, do a drill, but above all, don't just ignore it.

Remember what keeps your attention. In most cases, if you find a style or topic boring, so will your audience. What makes you pay attention and listen? Watch audience responses in church, at a concert, or while you are a part of the class. When are you paying attention the best? Most of us will listen intently during stories. We all listen to and laugh at good jokes. Trivia, anecdotes and obscure information will often recapture our attention. Knowing that these tools work on you, use them on your class.

Keep it fresh. The longer you teach a class or subject, it becomes tempting to just pull out the previous year's notes or outline and teach it again. Each year, another layer of staleness and mildew settles into the lecture. You don't have to rewrite your presentations from scratch every time, but adding a fresh story, reworking an outline with an alliteration, injecting some fresh research or visuals will make the material fresher to you and may inspire you to present the information with more vitality and personal interest.

Be succinct. One of the impacts of today's option-filled and readily available communication buffet is a shortened attention span. Sitcoms tear apart and rebuild relationships in twenty-two minutes flat. We can read an executive summary of an entire book while we are waiting for the plane to take off. Voice mails and emails allow us to communicate in two minutes or two paragraphs. Today's teacher, preacher, and lecturer must realize that we have to tell them what we are going to tell them, tell them and tell them what we told them swiftly and concisely. Otherwise, we'll lose them. In reality, it is more difficult to be succinct than it is to be verbose. Chose your words carefully and make each one count.

We've actually only just begun to scratch the surface of styles of communication in this chapter, but you've got a good start on improving your communication to your class, audience, faculty, and congregation. Styles vary and fluctuate, but they are essential to teaching information in such a way that it will be retained.

The old adage states that "you can lead a horse to water, but you can't make him drink." That is most likely true. But if you'll put a salt tablet under that old horse's tongue for a few minutes before you take him to the watering trough, by the time you walk him to the water; he'll be ready to drink long and deep. We cannot force our listeners to drink in every word we say. But we can create a thirst for knowledge, application, and information that will cause them to pay a little closer attention and hear what we have to say. And sometimes, enticing those kids to drink deeply from the well of knowledge, we will have moved out of our routines and will have begun to communicate with style.

Chapter Five

Deliver Your Excellence to Their Door Step

"Being excellent is one thing. Communicating excellence is another. Develop something worth talking about and then talk about it!"
—Philip C. Johnson, Ph.D.

School to Home Communication

Those who are involved in education know that the home is an essential link in the communication grid. Insufficient communication between the school and the home will always create tensions and problems that will ultimately eclipse your ultimate goals of educating students and changing lives.

Educators must realize that all communication directed toward the home needs to be actively clear in order to minimize potential miscommunications. Educators who have taught for as few as two days understand that much of what is said in the classroom occasionally goes home repackaged. Students sit around the dinner table sharing with parents that their Bible teacher taught them that Pharaoh forced the Hebrews slaves to make bread without straw, that David fought against Goliath, a giant "Finkelstein" and that Solomon had three hundred wives and seven hundred porcupines!

Misunderstandings happen. Sometimes we're not clear. Sometimes the student is not listening. Sometimes families simply misinterpret. We won't eradicate the specter of miscommunication in our lifetime, but we can all do our part to work for a "cure." While we communicate many things throughout the course of a day, one item that we always want to make sure gets delivered to the home with some measure of accuracy is the excellence factor of our ministries.

You Can't Just Sit Around

Schools come in all kinds of shapes and sizes. Different schools have unique personalities that can appeal to different people and can effectively meet the various needs of families. One thing that all schools have in common is the need to communicate excellence to the families that they serve. Parents want to know that the school they have chosen for their child is going to be a place dedicated to quality. In order to do this a school must assess several things: What are our ministry's areas of excellence? What are our ministry's weaknesses? How can we minimize and address the weaknesses and how can we effectively communicate our strengths?

A school starts its long journey towards excellence in the mind of a person or a group of people. Begin by making a wish list. Dream a little bit. Get together with your colleagues and brainstorm. Visit other Christian schools in your area and begin accumulating a list of ideas that you can use to make your school better. The dreaming stage can be invigorating and inspiring. It takes a vision of excellence to eventually produce qualities of excellence in your school.

At this point, some will focus on the multitude of things that need to be done or all that could be done in their particular institution. It is easy to become overwhelmed, discouraged or impatient by expecting to do too much too quickly. This often results in accomplishing nothing and the institution ends up treading educational water. Experienced educators know that you can dream big—sometimes ridiculously big—but they also know that you can only bite off a little bit at a time.

After dreaming and wishing (and then coming back to reality), start developing a plan and start making strides in the right direction. True, you may not be able to accomplish all that was on your "wish list," but any movement in the right direction will create pockets of excellence where there were once holes of mediocrity. The important thing is to start moving. People respond to movement and activity and it will cause them to perceive that things are headed in the right direction. The perception that you are moving will do wonders for your reputation and will begin to communicate excellence to your community. You don't have to have all of the bells and whistles to make things look good or at least to make things look better. Situations don't need to be perfect to start smelling excellent.

Several years ago there was a news report about a man by the name of Larry Walters. Larry was a fan of aviation. He had always wanted to fly so he joined the air force, but due to his poor eyesight, he was destined to stay on the ground. Larry's brief stint in the air force did not provide him with the opportunities to soar the heavens.

After being discharged from the air force and tired of being content to watch jets fly overhead, Larry decided to take matters into his own hands. He went to an Army-Navy

Surplus store and purchased forty weather balloons. Now, these were not party balloons designed to fascinate a group of six-year-old girls. These were heavy-duty balloons that were four feet across!

Larry attached these balloons to his favorite lawn chair. He kept the chair anchored to his pickup truck as he proceeded to gather his gun and his ice chest filled with sandwiches and drinks. The gun was for later. Larry figured that when he tired of flying, he would simply shoot a few of the balloons and waft gently back to earth.

When he was all situated, he cut himself loose and was on his way. But instead of floating gently up into the air, Larry shot up as if he had been fired from a cannon. And instead of leveling off at a couple of hundred feet, he finally stopped rising when he reached an altitude of fourteen thousand feet! At this point, the whole "shoot a couple of balloons" idea didn't seem too wise, so Larry had to just hold tight.

A passing airplane radioed back to the control tower that they had passed a guy in a lawn chair at fourteen thousand feet. The air traffic controller probably just made a note to cut back on that pilot's flight hours.

Finally Larry was noticed as he continued floating around in his lawn chair, snacking on sandwiches and drinking root beer. He arrived safely back on solid ground with the aid of a helicopter and crew and he was greeted by the media and the authorities ready to take him off to jail. (I guess he had forgotten about those pesky FAA guidelines that would generally prohibit flying lawn chairs from interfering with the air space of Los Angeles International Airport.)

Just before being taken away, one of the reporters asked Mr. Walters why he did it—why did he try to fly in a lawn chair? His answer? Simple . . . *"Well, a man can't just sit around . . ."*

We can take a lesson from Larry. We may not have the wherewithal to make every one of our school-related dreams an immediate reality, but we can certainly do "something." If we're going to see our vision accomplished, we can't just "sit around."

Key Areas Where Excellence Can Be Communicated

When you begin the task of beefing up the quality of your programs, or perhaps just the task of communicating how great your programs already are, it's important to focus on areas that are crucial. If you spend all of your energies promoting and talking about the wonders of your after-school clogging club, but ignore your school's stand for spiritual depth, you are missing the point. (I humbly ask the clogging community to forgive me if I have offended.) The following areas provide wonderful opportunities to communicate to parents the truly good things that you are doing.

Spiritual growth goals. What are your chapels like? Do they contain variety and solid content? Do they involve students and guest speakers? Do you invite parents to attend chapels or special spiritual emphasis assemblies? Quality chapels can communicate to families that spiritual growth is at the top of your list of priorities.

Take your students on mission trips. When you do, tell people. Let the students show their slides and tell their stories of the lives they impacted and how their own lives were changed.

Include spiritual highlights in your regular school correspondence. It's not enough to just brag about who won the last football game. Let parents know that students have made decisions for Christ, shared their faith and surrendered their lives.

Academics. Do you publish your standardized test scores? If not, why? If you're doing a credible job of academically training your students, then it will be reflected in standardized testing. Let parents know how well your school is doing compared to national averages.

Communicate to parents how many of your students get on the various types of honor rolls. Have awards ceremonies that honor outstanding academic achievement. Talk about the colleges that accept your graduates. Share about the scholarships that are awarded to your students. Let parents know in as many ways as possible that the education their child is receiving at your hands is going to prepare them for any service God would have for their lives. But do not allow your parents to get the impression that your school stands for excellent academics as an end in and of itself. Always link your training with preparation for a yielded student to be used of God for His honor and glory.

Newsletters. Newsletters provide an opportunity to do more than just convey information. Everything from the formatting to the font you chose says something about your organization, your quality and your style. If you want to communicate excellence, make sure you invest in a good desktop publishing program. Be creative! Make your publications eye-catching. And for goodness sakes, use the spell check! And it's always a good idea to have someone proofread your work as even the mighty spell checker can't tell what you *meant* to write or what you *wanted* to say.

Manuals, handbooks, and information packets. Call a couple of Christian schools and ask them to send you a sample packet of the information they circulate about themselves. Take a good long look at how their manuals and handbooks look. Now look at yours. Embarrassing isn't it? So, snatch a few ideas. They probably got their ideas from someone else themselves. There's very little that's totally original or new under the sun. See what ideas you can use to spruce up the look or content of your written materials. You want information that will look professional and attractive. You want it to be well organized and easy to understand. When you have quality materials, it conveys that you take details seriously. It will make a difference in the way students, parents and even prospective teachers perceive your school ministry.

Website. If your school doesn't have a website, you need to get one. They are one of the most cost effective ways of advertising your school, and they are wonderful tools for communicating excellence in quality.

A website can contain volumes of interesting information about your school and its programs. Here are some things to include and some things to take into consideration while designing the site:

- Make the site attractive and user friendly. Sometimes too many graphics will cause the page to load slowly. People will get bored and visit another sight.
- Include your school's mission statement in a prominent place.
- Include pictures of the school's administrative and teaching staff. (That's provided that you don't have a particularly frightening-looking staff. Go with your strengths.)
- Have different sections that highlight your spiritual emphasis, academics, fine arts and sports programs.
- Highlight student achievement on the site.

- If teachers have email addresses, have them listed on the sight.
- Include the school's calendar and lunch menu.
- Have special "revolving" pages that include outstanding student work, such as essays, poems or artwork.
- Include information for enrollment procedures.
- Highlight future plans for growth and development.
- Include links to other helpful sites.

Athletic programs. We could say that if you want to communicate excellence in the area of athletics, just win as many games as possible. But there is much more that goes into communicating excellence in a sports program. Areas to address are:
- Communication to parents about try-out procedures and requirements.
- Clear information regarding home and away games as well as locations and directions to those games.
- Standards regarding academic and behavior requirements for playing on teams.
- Training athletes to compete graciously under pressure, including a procedure for dealing with those who are taken out of a game for misconduct.
- Teaching students to win and lose gracefully.
- Balancing student understand that games can enhance life, but they are not life.

Social programs. Another opportunity to showcase your school's excellence is through your "social" activities. These include special parent lunch days, Thanksgiving feasts, grandparents' days, skate nights, school picnics, and the like. They allow a chance for families to get to know parts of your school and staff in a more informal setting.

Correspondence and phone calls. It is always a mark of excellence to make sure that correspondence is given prompt attention as well as returning phone calls. Often it is a good idea to set a certain time of day to handle all correspondence. If you have set times to respond to written requests and comments, you are more likely to keep from being overwhelmed with the task. If the correspondence is pressing, or perhaps deals with a homework assignment or behavioral problem, it is always advisable to respond immediately. Doing so communicates to parents that you are organized, thoughtful, efficient, and have their child's best interest at heart.

Likewise, with phone calls, it is best to reserve a time during the day when you will attend to the phone messages you have received. This can sometimes be your least favorite task because it holds so many variables. What did the caller want? What will their mood be? Will I be able to answer their questions and satisfy them? Will the phone call take an ugly turn and escalate into a shouting match? Yes, so many variables. But it's got to be done, so do it and keep the following principles in mind:

- You are a professional.
- Professionals care about others.
- Professionals try to help others and meet their needs.
- Professionals don't scream at others on the phone.

School programs. Christmas programs, Easter pageants, kindergarten graduations, high school graduations, special school appreciation programs: they all shout potential when it comes to publicly showcasing the innate qualities of your school. Think of it: you've got kids on a stage, a theme to center the action around, and parents in the seats, perhaps even a spotlight. What more could you ask for. Pound for pound the school program offers more opportunities to highlight the qualities of your school than any other avenue. Here are some things to keep in mind before the show goes on.

Always present with confidence. Confidence implies preparation and qualified staff members. No one finds it appealing to spend thousands of dollars a year to send their children to a school where the leaders are timid and unsure of their skills.

Start preparations early. Preparing early lends itself to a program with fewer glitches. It also significantly reduces your stress level and the stress level of those who come into contact with you.

Pay attention to length. Not too long ago I sat through what I had anticipated as being a very charming school program. A word to the wise: nothing is charming after more than two full hours. Actually it stopped being charming after the first hour and fifteen minutes. To make matters worse, it was a Grandparent's Day program and after the first hour the attendees kept getting up to use the bathroom and to exercise their newly replaced hips.

Outfits and costumes. It's amazing what a little imagination can do. It is also amazing how delighted parents become when they see their kids dressed up with little gray mouse ears. (That is with the exception of graduating high school seniors. From what I know of those who tried to adorn their seniors with animal costumes . . . well, let's just say, the reviews weren't good.)

Flow. It's important to keep the program moving. Provide guests with a well-designed and informative program and you will rid yourself of the need to explain everything as well as the need to introduce each student or group. Let the program speak for itself as much as possible.

Student involvement. The more students that you involve in your productions the more families you will have in attendance. And having more families in attendance means that more people will be blessed and will hear your message of excellence.

COMMUNICATING THE TEACHER'S IMAGE

In conclusion, it's important to realize that a school's strongest or weakest link in communicating excellence to the home may be the classroom teacher. The majority of a family's contact with the school comes through the classroom teacher. The following areas should be given attention in order to maximize their potential to communicate the best things to the home:

Bulletin boards. Make them shine. Make them warm. Make them thought provoking. Think of them as the billboards of your classroom advertising your strengths.

Class parties. Parties are the true test of a classroom teacher's control. If you can control your class in the presence of stray parents, cupcakes and games, you can control them anywhere. This can be an ideal opportunity to showcase your organizational and discipline abilities.

Teacher correspondence. Do you want parents to think that you're on top of things? Make sure you respond quickly to their written or phoned in request. Also, accurate spelling and correct grammar are always a nice touch!

Handling discipline situations. People do watch. It is a scientific fact that parents see far more student behavior on the playground while driving by at fifty miles per hour than three trained teachers see while standing ten feet away from students. It's important for teachers to stay alert. When handling a discipline situation or even reminding students of proper habits, always check your tone of voice. Avoid sarcasm or loud tones. It is also wise to know exactly where your hands are. Misunderstandings can happen so easily if you're not careful. I know of a teacher who raised his hand up in front of him to ask a student to be quiet. At the same time the student stuck out his tongue. Wet, sticky tongue collided with outstretched hand and there was very definitely a difference in how that incident was interpreted. The student's view was that the teacher smacked him. The teacher's view was that the student licked him. Often it's best to keep your hands behind you so that you won't be misunderstood.

Report card comments. In an age where everything, including report card comments can be automated, it's important to remember that nothing replaces the well thought out, hand-written comment.

Greetings. Your first and final chance to leave parents with a quality impression is in the morning when students arrive and in the afternoon when they get in their cars. In the morning is the time for warm greetings and an encouraging word. It's not the time for a long conference. By your tone and attitude you can communicate that each student is getting ready to embark upon the most important educational day of their lives. In the afternoon, as students leave your room or get into their parent's cars, you have your last chance to communicate to parents that you love their child and are looking forward to doing it all over again the next day.

Being excellent is one thing. Communicating excellence is another. Develop something worth talking about and then talk about it!

Chapter Six

Communication Starts at the Top: The Pastor's Communication and a Word for School Boards

"It is important that the pastor be viewed as the primary (but not sole) spiritual leader of the school."

—Dan Burrell, Ed.D.

Please allow me to be rather personal in this chapter. I hope that schoolteachers and school administrators will read this in addition to the pastors of churches that have Christian schools. It has been my privilege to serve as pastor of two churches both of which had large Christian schools. My first ministry saw our school grow from a little over three hundred students to nearly seven hundred students. My current school has over eleven hundred students in it. Because I am a graduate of Christian schools, because I have training in education, because I know the effects of public education and its entrenched secular philosophy, and because I have been in the classroom and behind the pulpit, my perspectives and opinions on pastoral leadership and communication in the Christian school run deep.

Quite frankly, I am concerned that many pastors of churches that sponsor Christian schools are missing a tremendous opportunity in their Christian school. I am also concerned that there is a dangerous spirit of competition in many ministries that pits the school against the church as they assign resources and distribute available dates on the calendar. This has created an attitude that ranges from antagonism to outright hostility in some ministries and such is not healthy for the Body of Christ, the Church, or the School.

I'm afraid that well-educated teachers and administrators intimidate many pastors. I've watched as pastors have felt the pain of families who chose to leave the church when something didn't go right with their kids in the school. They have felt like a fifth wheel at many school functions not really knowing their place or role. They are so busy with other aspects of the ministry that they have relegated nearly all of the leadership to the school administration and have lost touch with the heart and joy of Christian education.

I've also seen school administrators become frustrated with a lack of recognition for the spiritual mission of their work. Teachers who have become burned-out as they become unpaid but conscripted volunteers in open church ministry are common. There is the constant frustration of a classroom left neatly on Friday afternoon that mysteriously becomes "trashed" after a week-end of youth activities and Sunday school classes.

I want to encourage pastors, administrators and classroom teachers alike to renew their commitment to three specific things. First, a renewed commitment to good communication between the pastor and the school. Second, a renewed commitment to good communication between the church and school. Third, a renewed commitment to the real goal of Christian education: to reach boys and girls for Jesus Christ and to see them grow up in the knowledge and application of His Word. Let me give you a few thoughts on a variety of subjects that relate to these three concerns:

THE PASTOR NEEDS TO TAKE THE LEAD

From one pastor to another, the senior pastor of the church has the privilege, opportunity and *responsibility* to provide leadership for the school. It is dishonest to take a church with a Christian school then starve it to death with inattention or constricted resources.

It frustrates me to see pastors miss the opportunity they have in their school, but it seems to almost be a point of amusement for some. Several years ago I was in Nashville, Tennessee at a conference for pastors and I overheard a conversation that went something like this, "Say, I hear you are a candidate for the senior Pastor position at XYZ church in 'Topeka'." "Well, yes I am." "Don't they have a Christian school at that church?" "Are you kidding? Does it look like I've lost my mind? I'd never want to pastor a church with a Christian school!" They both chortled as they went on their way. I can't imagine that we would speak in such derogatory terms about the Sunday school or choir or deaf ministry. Why would such a stigma be placed on having a Christian school?

Yes, the Christian school brings unique challenges and problems to a local church. But it will also provide many blessings. I believe that Satan only attacks those ministries that threaten what he is doing. Can you imagine how unleashing wave after wave of sharp, well-educated, philosophically sound young people must frighten him? Of course, he will oppose it! Of course there will be conflicts. But is it worth it? Absolutely!

The senior pastor must believe in and support the Christian school. He doesn't have to be a professional educator. He doesn't have to understand curriculum and pedagogy.

But he should care about the spiritual quality, the character content, and the eternal direction of those who spend forty hours a week on the campus of the church. The pastor needs to be involved. Toward that end, allow me to suggest ten things a pastor can do to communicate his leadership in the school:

- Be a part of new teacher orientation.
- Take part in parent orientation.
- Speak in chapel regularly and attend frequently.
- Attend some of the faculty meetings.
- Walk through the halls regularly.
- Minister to school families who are in need.
- Attend the teacher's convention with the staff.
- Participate in student and staff retreats.
- Mention his involvement in and support for the school from the pulpit.
- Be a pastor to the staff and faculty.

The school administration needs to support the pastor.

Sure, sometimes you have to explain things to the pastor because he doesn't understand educational lingo. And yes, there is always the danger of politics within a ministry as you handle unruly students or a disgruntled family. But it is imperative to remember that God established the Church as one of three institutions for human well-being: church, home, and state. In a church/school setting, the church has priority and not *vice versa*.

Allow me to suggest ten things an administrator can do to connect the pastor to the school:

- Keep him in the information loop. Meet with him at least once a week and update him more frequently as needed.

- Understand his vision and goals for the school and see that it is implemented.
- Promote the church through the school.
- Invite him to all functions, but recognize he won't be able to attend them all.
- Involve him with the students personally by asking him to spend time with them.
- Protect him from controversy. Allow him to remain the pastor while you enforce the policies.
- Recognize that his ministry encompasses more than the day school and respect his need for addressing those other areas of ministry.
- Don't make decisions that will impact him or the church without seeking his counsel first.
- Be a team player when requesting resources and calendar dates.
- Encourage the staff, faculty and school families to be active in the church.

Find keys areas for pastoral leadership. It is important that the pastor be viewed as the primary (but not sole) spiritual leader of the school. There are a few events each year that really require a pastor's involvement if he is to be effective in establishing his leadership in the school which will allow him to communicate the truth to the listener. It is my recommendation that the pastor should do his best to attend and speak at least briefly at the following events:
- New teacher orientation
- Returning teacher orientation
- Parent orientation
- At least one Parent/Teacher Fellowship
- All graduations

- At least four chapel services per year
- At least one in-service workshop per year
- The annual Christmas concert or program
- At least four faculty meetings per year

As a pastor, I have found that this is most likely to happen when I schedule these events on my personal calendar prior to the beginning of the school year. I usually over-schedule events such as chapels so that I can have room to rearrange them when events conflict.

Be willing to promote the church through the school. Pastors, administrators and teachers should all have the goal of seeing boys and girls accept Christ and for the families to be regularly involved in a good local church. Churches and schools that have a strategy for reaching unchurched families can see tremendous blessings as entire families accept Christ. Here are some ways to communicate to school families about the things that are going on in the church:

- Place school families on the church mailing list. Let them know of upcoming church events that may be of interest to them.
- Let the pastor and his pastoral staff know about school students or parents who are in the hospital so a quick visit can be made when they make hospital visits.
- Have the pastor or administrator make a brief mention of upcoming church events that may be of interest to school families like marriage seminars or child-rearing classes. This can be done at public meetings or in newsletters.
- Have the church and school websites interconnected and intricately linked. There should be multiple crosswalks between both websites.

- Encourage the pastoral staff to be supportive of school functions for the purpose of ministering and networking. Many relationships are started at school picnics, baseball games, or science fairs.

Everyone Must Commit to Making Church and School Conflicts Minimal

Let's admit it, there are going to be multiple, even numerous conflicts between the church and the school. Many times these are the result of inadequate communication between the church and school. Here are a few suggestions for improving communication which would avoid some of these conflicts.

Have the school headmaster or administrator in pastoral staff meetings. He or she certainly is leading one of the most important and perhaps even the largest ministries of the church and should be at the table when the overall planning for the ministry is taking place.

Have a calendar strategy. There won't be enough nights in the year to put all ballgames, youth activities, revival services, etc. So develop a reasonable calendar schedule (which must contain some flex in it) to assist you, by assigning a certain number of Friday nights each month to each ministry, reserving key events on the calendar like Orientation night or Missions Conference, and developing a system for reserving rooms, dates and resources for all events.

Don't tolerate behind-the-scenes grumbling. Everyone must commit to avoiding and dealing with gossiping and back-biting that creates tension between the church and school ministries. This is counter-productive and wrong.

Use an "in-house" communication tool. At our ministry, we call it the "Loop" and its purpose is to let the right hand know what the left hand is doing as much as possible. It doesn't contain every bit of information, but it is a part of the process of encouraging good communication between ministry arms.

Assume the best. Sometimes the best thing we can do is be positive and not cynical. Even if things are confusing or a conflict is occurring, leadership can contain the problem or exacerbate it by how they respond to it. Don't mutter under your breath about the "over-bearing church" or the "resource-sucking school" and simply put on a smile and say, "Well, this is going to be a challenge, but I'm sure we'll work something out!" Because, in the end, you will have to work something out and it is wrong to pollute or discourage others with a wrong attitude.

The Board-run School and the Chairman of the Board

Finally, I'd like to make a few comments for board-run schools and to the chairman of the school board in particular. Many times board members are successful businessmen and women, long-term school family members and have made significant contributions to the school in terms of time and resources. Your communication with the staff, parents and students is also essential. Here are a few ideas which may make your communication cleaner and more effective as well:

Develop trust and encourage communication between the board and the administration. The relationship between the board and the administration should not be adversarial.

A breakdown in trust leads to a breakdown in communication which leads to a breakdown in leadership. Sometimes it is good to have communication that is separate from the formal board setting. Have open lines of communication that can be accessed between board meetings as well.

Regularly update the staff, parents, and students as to the mission, strategy, and goals for the school. As staff and students turnover, it cannot be assumed that the new wave understands (or even agrees with) what the Christian school is all about. It is incumbent upon the board to protect and promote the overall mission of the Christian school ministry.

Let the chairman speak for the board. Few things complicate communication more than too many voices speaking for the whole. When difficult decisions are made, policy changes are implemented or a vision is unveiled, it is best to allow one person, generally the chairman, speak for the board. The rest of the board can then support and encourage the leader as he or she communicates what they have agreed to as a group.

Be supportive. If you can't be supportive, then perhaps you shouldn't be on the board. This doesn't mean that you shouldn't take a stand against wrong-doing. But it does mean that when you don't get your way on an issue or two, you still walk out of the board meeting supportive of the decisions reached. I have always appreciated board members who have stated their objections or concerns privately, but once the vote was taken and we were in public, they supported the decision with unity. That takes character and always earns my respect.

Avoid being reactive. It is dangerous to make decisions too quickly or without doing your homework very carefully. Impulsive decisions are often unwise decisions. Use thoughtful and prayerful deliberation. Consult counsel. Listen to the administration—they are the ones who are in the trenches each day and who must implement the will of the board. There are few decisions that must be made the same night they are proposed.

Show appropriate respect to those in the meeting. This goes both ways. I've seen over-educated administrators treat board members like dirty-necked yokels. I've also seen board members request a report from an over-worked administrator who prepared for his presentation for hours only to have some members doze off during the presentation or wave him on as if they are bored. Beyond the obvious rudeness of such action, it undermines the confidence and respect that should exist between the board and the administration.

Cast a vision. The board not only provides accountability and counsel, but vision and cheerleading. It is essential that the school board be viewed as in touch, positive and proactively involved in the future development of the school ministry. Reticence, apathy, or discouragement will create instability and will create the sensation of drift or worse. Consider having an emphasis point for all board members to promote and emphasize as they leave the meeting. This will create a positive "stir" across the campus as the vision is spread.

Dr. Lee Roberson, the great *pastor emeritus* of Highland Park Baptist Church in Chattanooga, Tennessee and the founder of Tennessee Temple Schools has often said, "Everything rises and falls on leadership." How the pastoral and board leadership communicates will very often determine the effectiveness of their leadership.

Chapter Seven

Communicating Through the Iron Curtain: Administators and Teachers

"If we can learn to accurately communicate our hearts to one another, we will more than likely find more gratification in working together."

—Philip C. Johnson, Ph.D.

History as well as American culture is rife with examples of arch rivalries: David had his Goliath, Superman had his Lex Luther, Tom had his Jerry. Then there's the relationship between administrators and teachers. OK, so perhaps there are no slingshots involved, and maybe no one is chasing anyone with the intent to eat them for a snack, but at some level, the contention still exists from time to time.

The struggle between those who teach and those who administrate is not new. To varying degrees, there can be underlying misunderstandings between these two groups that can thwart positive communication and harmonious working relationships. Teachers sometimes believe that administrators have forgotten what it's like to work in the trenches of the classroom. Administrators are sometimes frustrated with the choices and actions of the classroom teachers, believing them to be unsympathetic towards the nuts and bolts efforts that occur behind the classroom stage and incapable of grasping the big picture.

Some would assume that situations involving Christians working together in a Christ-honoring ministry would preempt the existence of conflict. But those of us who live in the real world know that sharing a common bond in Jesus does not always mean that we get along. However, because we *are* Christians and *should* be working toward the same goal, we ought to be motivated to understand each other and to communicate in such a way that will promote harmony and effective service. If we can learn to accurately communicate our hearts to one another, we will more than likely find more gratification in working together.

For the Administrator

Communicate what you value. What is important to administrators? Enrollment? After all, you've got to keep the numbers up if you're going to be able to pay the teachers, and you certainly don't want to be embarrassed when other administrators ask you how your enrollment is coming along, right?

Or maybe you find value in your bottom line finances. That is important because otherwise you'll have to start shutting down certain programs, and people will lose their jobs, and students may find another school. That, of course, would lead to a smaller enrollment, and well, we've already talked about that.

Is it prestige, influence, or power that gets you out of bed in the morning? What? You're shocked? You're asking who in Christian service could ever be lured by this mistress? Hmm . . . probably more than you'd think. Christian service is not immune to performance-based motivation or the subtle call of glory. It's just a different pond with different fish.

Perhaps the thing that is most important to some administrators is peace and quiet. Just let things sail along. Let the teachers solve their own problems. Don't mess with enrollment. Don't toy with my finances. Tell parents I'm in a meeting. Just don't bother or inconvenience me!

Or maybe you're one of those old-fashioned administrators who is concerned about student development, spiritual growth, family relationships, and preparing students to meet the demands of the future.

In my experience of dealing with and speaking to teachers about this issue, they often communicate that they are frustrated with administrators who don't specifically share what they value, and sometimes inadvertently communicate disturbing values.

Granted, administration by the very nature of the job requires someone to be concerned about enrollment numbers, finances, group insurance rates, and law suits. Unfortunately, those necessary concerns can sap time and energy away from communicating other things that should be our primary concerns, such as the spiritual and academic development of students. Therefore, administrators must be proactive in their communication of values. In other words, *plan* to communicate your heart-values on purpose.

Talk about it. Use part of your staff meetings to share what's important to you. Don't miss opportunities to remind your staff of your spiritual mission. Let teachers know from your own lips what is the real bottom line: making a difference for all eternity.

Write about it. Put your goals and objectives for your particular Christian school in writing in your brochures, in your handbooks and in your newsletters home to parents. Let the message be fully integrated in your school literature. This provides not only a good reminder to parents, students and teachers, it is also a good reminder for administrators.

Live it. Teachers can tell when you're just giving lip service to the issue. They need to know that principle, quality, and spiritual values are at the heart of what you do. But what is it that they observe? Do they hear you talk about changing lives and then see you throwing a temper tantrum over losing a prominent family and their precious tuition? Do others see you agonizing over lost money or the lost opportunity to reach a family for Christ? Our actions often do speak much more loudly than words.

Communicate support. I have asked large numbers of teachers the following question: If you could have all the classroom supplies and resources that you could possibly want, or you could have administrative support, which would you choose? The answer is always the same: administrative support. Administrative support is crucial to teachers. It is what teachers appreciate most.

When should administrative support towards teachers occur? Three times: before, during, and after a problem. Teachers need to feel that they can count on administrative support early in the school year, *before* any problems arise. This gives them security and confidence to proceed and to put their lives and hearts into their jobs.

Support should continue *during* any problems that should arise. It is devastating to a staff member to find out that administrative support waffles when a difficulty becomes a reality. Let's face it, sometimes it's simply easier to put the blame on the teacher or take the side of a parent in a sticky situation. Sometimes the path of least resistance is taken, forgetting that doing things right is not often the easiest way. It may be more convenient for you at the time, but it will cost the administrator significantly in lost credibility.

And support should continue *after* the problem has been resolved. Regardless of the outcome of any given situation, the teacher needs to know that the administrator has a continued desire to support the teacher and help him continue to develop into a master teacher.

Obviously there are times when a teacher or staff member truly makes a mistake and puts the school and the administration in a very awkward situation. It happens. But depending on the seriousness of the offense and the heart-response of the teacher, it is possible to recover from these missteps and doing so will often provide growth for all who are involved. Here are some gracious ways to deal with these situations:

- Don't show lack of support for erring teachers in front of parents or students.
- If you're caught off guard by an angry (and possibly justifiably indignant parent), don't panic. Use a phrase similar to this: "I'll be happy to look into this for you." Or, "Let me get all of the facts and I'll get back in touch with you." When we act too quickly or allow others to rush us in our decisions, we sometimes end up doing and saying things that we will end up regretting.
- If you find that a teacher has erred in judgment or procedure, deal with the issue privately.
- If you have a teacher who has made a poor or unwise decision but responds to the correction well, be prepared to forgive and restore. Let it go and move on.
- If the offense is serious enough (or repetitious enough) to warrant dismissal, there is still no reason to be anything less than gracious. The kindest communication would include straight-forward honesty and, depending on the circumstances,

pointing the individual in the direction of someone who could provide some help.

Communicate with your presence. An administrator's physical presence is often more important than he or she realizes. Here are a few places the administrator needs to make a regular appearance.

Be in the classrooms. This sounds so fundamental. But many administrators and principals find that their schedules become increasingly busier and one day they look up and realize that it's been two months since they were last in a classroom. The classroom is where the action takes place. It is where you can evaluate the skills and abilities of your teachers. Your presence there communicates that you're interested in the quality of the academics that occur.

Be in the lunchroom. Lunchroom tables, food, gregarious conversations going on at unacceptable decibel levels . . . Who wouldn't want to be there? This is an ideal opportunity to get to know the students on a different level. It is also a good place to hear very interesting conversations . . . some of which may need your input.

Go to some ballgames. Attending athletic events shows support for the school and the students. It also allows more casual interaction with teachers, parents and students.

Attend church/school social engagements. If you do it right, you can show off your fun, lighthearted side during group social situations while still maintaining your carefully crafted dignity.

Go to the room or office of the employees. Take a lesson from Abraham Lincoln. When he needed to visit his generals, he often visited them on their turf, in their tents. Do not always summons your teachers to your "throne" room. Visiting teachers in their classrooms communicates accessibility, thoughtfulness and that you're interested in a connection to their lives and their concerns.

Communicate even when you're busy. Of course you're busy. And if you weren't busy, you'd never admit it. For some reason, our culture has placed a very high premium on the act of being "busy." Somehow, one's busy-ness quotient signifies value and worth. Just for fun, next time someone asks you how things are going, instead of saying that you're tremendously busy and four to six weeks from seeing the light of day, try this statement, "Oh, I'm doing fine. Watching a lot of TV." Watch their mouths drop open as you admit to having some free time to enjoy a smidgen of fun.

Truth be told, however, administrators do often have many irons in the fire and they need to be creative in their communication to their schools during particularly hectic times.

Try speaking for just five minutes at a staff meeting. You may not be needed to run a routine meeting, but you are needed to put your special touch on the meeting. In five minutes you can share a spiritual truth, enhance the tone, set some vision and remind your staff that you are actively in charge of leading them.

Do a quick campus walk-through. Breeze through a few rooms everyday. Don't plan on camping out, just walk through. You'd be surprised what you learn and what you catch. Doing this communicates to your teachers and students that you are just a little bit unpredictable and that you're liable to show up at any given moment. It tends to keep people pleasantly on guard, and honest.

Write a short note of appreciation. Even in the midst of deadlines and pressures, administrators need to make sure that they offer praise to their staff. Keep a supply of blank cards in your desk and develop an eye for spotting good things. When you do make a pleasant observation, write a quick note letting the individual know that you have noticed. Often we are far better at noting the negatives than in noting the positives.

Offer a 30-second, in-person compliment. A well-deserved, well-stated compliment can communicate volumes and generally helps the one who receives it to survive until at least Spring Break.

Make good use of the memo. A memo referencing procedures or upcoming events reminds your staff that though you may be busy, you are still very much aware of what is happening on your campus. Don't forget these general rules about writing memos:
- Keep it organized using titles and subtitles. Shockingly, not everyone reads every word of everything you write.
- End with a concise summary. See rule number one.
- Remember that clarity is more important than length.
- Remember, carelessly worded memos can breed misunderstandings. Facial expressions and voice inflections are not evident when someone is reading a memo.

For the Teacher

Communicate loyalty. There are many things that administrators look for in quality teachers. They want teachers who are spiritually mature, possess wonderful skills, have good relationships with parents and students, and teachers who are creative. But right at the top of the list of most-coveted character values is loyalty. Administrators want teachers who communicate that they are loyal to the school and to their leader in a variety of ways.

Communicate loyalty through your speech. Does the teacher actively speak well of the school and the administration? Administrators often face pressures and difficulties that are unknown to the teacher. Knowing and hearing of the teacher's loyalty communicates confidence and trust to the administrator.

Communicate loyalty by avoiding gossip. While many Christians shun more obvious sins, some still engage in this often-enjoyable social iniquity. Listening to gossip about your school or participating in gossip about the same, destroys your credibility and hurts the work of Christ as well as individuals. You may not be able to stop rumors from flying around, but everyone can make a choice about repeating them.

Communicate loyalty by turning in requested materials on time. This includes special projects, dated materials, informational forms, intent-to-return letters, and contracts. As I look back over my time in administration, I have always been encouraged by employees who eagerly and quickly return the paperwork that was assigned. It is especially encouraging to receive intent-to-return forms and contracts before the day that they are actually due.

Communicate support of school policies. Once you've signed a contract to teach for another year, choose to support the school policies. That does not mean that you have to agree with every little thing that goes on. If you have a big disagreement, you shouldn't have signed the contract. But if you have decided to sign, communicate support of school policies in the following ways:

- Don't make stray comments to students that disagree with school policy.
- Don't make stray comments to parents regarding the same.
- Don't reveal passive-aggressive behavior, agreeing with administration to their face and back-biting later.
- Be attentive during faculty meetings.

Communicate integrity. Administrators want teachers that they can trust. They have enough to worry about, what with Mrs. Hinkle's demands for a gifted program for her daughter who possesses an IQ of forty-two and Mr. Meyer's insistence on a sauna for the gym. They don't need to worry about you, too.

Watch your conduct. This involves your conduct in and out of the classroom. As a Christian educator, you must rise above selfish tendencies and understand that your life will be examined. That is a positive, not a negative. Teachers have an opportunity to impact eternity like few others.

Watch your tongue. Think before you talk. Don't say things that could potentially come back to haunt you and give your boss a headache. Be gentle with students, patient with parents, and longsuffering with co-workers.

Be honest in your teaching. Are you only at your best during the week of your yearly teacher evaluation? Honest teaching includes doing all the extras that make great teachers, even when you think no one is noticing. Your teaching can communicate volumes to your administrator when he breezes through your room. Are you sitting behind the desk? Are your students always bogged down with seatwork? Are you teaching passively? Honest teaching means teaching as consistently and as effectively as you can for the entire year.

Be a good steward of supplies. A final area of integrity is found in the way in which you handle school supplies. Often when we're not the ones who write the checks for items that we use every day we don't value them like we should. A teacher interested in communicating integrity is also a teacher who chooses to be a good steward of the things he uses. He does not waste but finds creative ways to use things again. He is careful to get the most mileage out of all that comes into his realm.

Communicate when you've got a gripe. You are going to run into situations where you will have valid gripes. I served as a classroom teacher for enough years to recognize this truth. But there is definitely a right way and a wrong way to go about dealing with difficult situations. The wrong way usually involves sarcasm, yelling, threatening revenge, and law suits followed by regrets later. The right way to deal with conflict includes the following:

Prayer. Always pray about issues before you confront anyone. Some issues are worth overlooking.

Come to your administration with the right attitude. If you come to express a concern when you don't have your emotions under control, you're liable to say many things that you never intended to say. Perhaps your concern is over the quality of the playground equipment. If you have allowed yourself to become emotionally overwrought over the monkey bars and safety issues, you might find yourself spouting off not only about the equipment, but also about the boss's toupee and love of plaid sports jackets—not a wise thing to mention, I assure you!

Come prepared to lose the fight. There is no guarantee that others will see things your way. No one will win all of his skirmishes and it is wise to understand this and allow yourself to remain in a position to lock horns later on a different issue if necessary. If you can't handle losing a fight, don't bother starting the battle.

Don't make demands or give ultimatums unless you're prepared to carry them out. If you threaten to quit, you'd better already have a job offer from the Christian Academy across the street.

Choose your battles carefully. You can't fight over everything. It's smarter to be strategic about how and when you will choose to disagree over any given issue. Will you fight for quality curriculum or will you argue over the ravioli they served for lunch? Those who fight over every little issue are often dismissed as complainers, and they lose any clout they might have had.

Purpose to keep an open mind that embraces the big picture of the ministry. Don't allow your own pet projects and self-centered desires to give you tunnel vision. No school revolves around one person or one program. When you embrace a bird's-eye view of the ministry as a whole, you may find you have less to be unhappy about.

Graciously accept the response from your current God-given authority. Your response is crucial. It is in your best interest to develop a relationship with your administration that allows you the luxury of sharing things freely. But that freedom often depends on how graciously you accept their decisions and their views of issues that are important to you. Employ grace and respect, and you'll survive to share again on another day!

Chapter Eight

Getting the Most from Your Methods: "Putting Power and Punch into Your Communication"

"From the moment you are recognized as the speaker or author, people have begun to form opinions. Opinions about you, whom you represent, what you are saying, and how they are going to respond."
—Dan Burrell, Ed.D.

I'm sure you've heard the advertising for the communication program called "Verbal Advantage" which has been on the radio for the last couple of decades. They remind us that people draw conclusions about us based on the words we use. The taped program promises to enhance our vocabulary in such a way that people will sit up and pay attention to us when we talk. In reality, this isn't just typical advertising hype, it is the truth.

Generally speaking, you will rarely offend someone by using interesting words, concise syntax, and correct grammar whether or not your audience is particularly educated or not. But stand in front of a group of college graduates and use monosyllabic words, mixed metaphors, and slaughter the King's English and you will have a large percentage of them shut you off before you ever reach your main point.

In addition, we communicate in a variety of ways beyond penning a few words or stating a few sentences. From the moment you are recognized as the speaker or author, people have begun to form opinions. Opinions about you, whom you represent, what you are saying, and how they are going to respond. There are multiple facets to communication that run the gamut from the words you actually use and how they are arranged to what you are wearing or whether or not you use four-color ink. You actually begin communicating to the parents of students from the moment they arrive on your campus if not before. Therefore, it is vitally important that you not only recognize how you are communicating, but *what* you are communicating.

The following is a list of general ideas for putting more power and punch into what and how you communicate. By applying some of these principles, you may find that people will listen closer to what you are communicating, will provide you with a greater response and hopefully, you will enhance your position as a leader in communication in your school. After all, if teachers and educational leaders aren't experts in communicating facts and ideas, then who would be? Here are some practical ideas for your consideration.

Make Sure You Leave the Impression That What You Are About to Communicate Is Important

This begins long before you will utter your first sentence or they read your first word. For example, if given a choice between reading something in black and white and two or more colors, I will almost always pick up the colored work. When I visit a church and the service appears to be disorganized, there is no prelude music, or the service starts late, I am left with the impression that someone isn't taking what he or she is doing very seriously. They certainly haven't prepared well for my arrival. It is very easy to become lacidasical about how we communicate to our constituents. This shows disrespect for both the audience and the message.

When making a speech before a large crowd . . .
Dress appropriately. That may mean putting on a suit and tie (when appearing before bankers or business executives.) It may mean taking a tie off or wearing casual slacks (when appearing before agricultural workers or blue-collar folks.) A general rule is to stay within the same range as the typical audience member, but at the high end. For example, if everyone is wearing ties, I'd probably at least start off with a tie and a jacket. If no one is wearing a tie, I'd probably start off with a tie and no jacket and might loosen the tie. This allows you to relate and still be distinguishable. Well-polished shoes, neatly groomed hair and fashionable clothing choices are additional non-negotiables for public speaking. Sometimes people complain about the expense of clothing for people who speak publicly, but this is part of the toolbox for effectiveness. The carpenter doesn't complain when he has to buy a hammer; he knows it is part of how he will get the job done. The educator should recognize that a good appearance will make him or her more effective.

Set the tone. Be early. Have the room well lighted. Check the sound system before anyone is in the audience. Have some prelude music playing as people enter. Mix and mingle with your audience for a few moments before you speak to emphasize your approachability and enhance your ability to relate. Double check all audio-visual equipment you will be using. Start off with a high-energy illustration that will capture their attention. Many people will make up their minds about whether or not they'll listen to you in the last few minutes preceding your presentation and the first few minutes of what you actually say. Once you have lost them, it is very difficult to recapture them.

Be Prepared. Don't be tied to notes. Never read your presentation (unless presenting an academic paper in a formal setting.) You should be so familiar with the material you are giving that you only need a guideline to keep you on track or to ensure accuracy.

Be Excited. If you aren't feeling well, fake it! If you aren't really excited about it, let someone else communicate it. You are the person responsible for getting the information across and if you don't appear to believe in what you are saying, the audience certainly won't either.

Be Prayed Up. Never forget that we are involved in a spiritual endeavor whenever we handle truth. Therefore, take a few moments and ask the Lord for clarity of thought, direction and effectiveness. Without the unction of His Holy Spirit, our words will fall wasted anyway.

Be Knowledgeable. You will never be smarter than everyone in the room on everything. But you should challenge every person in the room in one-way or another. Learn a few new words and add them to your presentation. Find interesting trivia that supports your thesis. Cite research that validates your conclusions. Add illustrations that make the information palatable and relatable.

When speaking to someone on a personal level . . .

Be approachable. By appearing to be too busy or too important to listen to others, you erect a wall that will be almost impossible to overcome. Make yourself reasonably available. Have scheduled times when you can meet with parents or talk on the phone. If someone catches you at a bad time, apologize profusely and ask them when it would be convenient for you to call them. This will go a long way in reassuring your parents that you care.

Be warm. Look people in the eye. Nod positively when appropriate. Even if you must deliver bad news, do so with compassion and warmth. Instruct without lecturing. Be firm without being cold. If they grow emotional, reassure them. If they grow angry or frustrated, redirect them by asking them to restate their concern in a more positive way. Warmness does not have to mean "softness." But there should always be an element of your communication that communicates compassion and Christlikeness.

Watch your posture. Body language speaks volumes. Folding your arms, tapping your fingers, looking over someone's head, or stiffness are all ways of negatively communicating without ever speaking a word. Tilt your head forward or to the side. Use your hands with small, close-to-the-body gestures. Conclude the conversation with a firm handshake or squeeze of the elbow when appropriate.

Be personal. Try to find a personal connection with the individual. Inquiry about their family. Learn names. Be empathetic. If you promise to follow up, do so. And it is a good idea to follow up on important conversations, even if they are impromptu.

When communicating through writing . . .

Proofread, proofread, proofread. One of the cardinal sins of the educator is to send out information that hasn't been proofread. Doing your own proofreading is next to impossible. You will often overlook your own mistakes. (There's a sermon in there, isn't there?) Have someone else proofread for grammar and technical errors.

Type it when necessary. As a general rule, formal communication should be typewritten. Personal communication may be hand written, but only if your handwriting is legible. Most word processing programs will also automatically spell-check your work and may even point out grammatical errors.

Be succinct. It is not necessary to write lengthy letters or articles when short ones will do. In fact, it is generally more difficult to write concisely than it is to be wordy.

Use appropriate vocabulary. Keep in mind to whom you are writing. Be willing to challenge your reader with a few new or challenging words. Don't overwhelm young or uneducated readers with big words in an effort to impress them. You'll come off like as arrogant or as a verbal bully.

Give Consideration to Your Audience

Putting parents into second-grade desks to endure a ninety-minute orientation presentation is not only cruel, but in some states it may be considered physical assault. Make sure that your room is clean, smells nice (take note preschool, kindergarten and biology teachers), that information is ready for distribution and that comfortable seating is provided. A nice touch can be some light refreshments or even a few mints or candies available for each listener. Don't assume that everyone will come prepared to take notes either. You may want to have some pencils and paper handy.

By using prepared notes and good use of your time, you should also make the meeting short and direct. Let them know that you respect their time and will make good use of the time. Allow those who have questions to remain afterwards, but dismiss those who would like to leave earlier. Don't hold your audience hostage by keeping them longer than is appropriate.

Recognize Non-verbal Communication

There are so many things that can communicate in a school setting. Walk on your campus, into your buildings, into each classroom pretending that this is your first time in each location. What do you notice first? Here are some questions to consider.

Is the campus clean and well-maintained? Have the lawn service scheduled to come right before major functions. Have someone do trash pickup detail hours before an event. Check light bulbs and restrooms. Is there adequate signage giving directions?

Is student work displayed? Is it displayed appropriately? Does the classroom look cluttered with too much work or too sparse with too little work? Have a variety of student work displayed. Make sure all students are represented. Avoid putting negative examples on display. Confine student displays to specific areas.

Are the bulletin boards relevant? Ah, the bane of the teacher's existence: the bulletin board. Too often, we fail to use this communication device effectively. Are they up-to-date? Do they have a clear message? Do they show creativity?

Is the room orderly? Is there excessive clutter? Make sure chairs are orderly. Provide a trash receptacle. Clean the chalkboards. Remove old bulletins from the bookracks. Do a quick "once over" for paper on the floor.

For printed material . . . .

Is the information accurate? Double-check the facts. Few things are more confusing than to have to correct misinformation.

Does it look appealing? There are many ways to add to the interest level of printed material. Use artwork, color, font variations or layout innovations to capture the interest of potential readers before they even pick up what you have written.

Is it available? Make a few extra copies of your best communication and spread them around. Have copies of your school newspaper in the church lobby or near the main desk at school. Put leftover copies of your school yearbook in local doctor's offices or car mechanic waiting rooms. Make sure the people answering the phone (and thereby answering questions) have copies of memos that have been sent home.

Spread the Good News

Don't be afraid to tell others what is going on in your school. Issue press releases. Make special t-shirts available for fun events that have your school name on them. Have bumper stickers for honor roll students, students of the month, or other honors. Encourage parents to promote the school by putting license plate holders or front plates on their cars. Don't be afraid to tell others what the Lord is doing in your ministry!

Make an Investment in Communication

You will need to recognize that money spent on improving communication is usually wisely spent. Don't try to do everything on the cheap. Don't be wasteful, but be willing to assign resources to making your ultimate job—communicating truth and information—more effective. Here are some places to assign financial resources if you've not already done so.

Communication technology. From video imagers to *Powerpoint®* programs, much technology that will enhance your communication is available.

Promotional Items. Have a refrigerator magnet calendar with important dates and the school name made and sent to every home as a gift. A modest, but appropriate Christmas gift for each family near the holidays is another idea.

Team Identity. Get each of your staff members a nice golf shirt with your school logo emblazoned on it to be worn on special occasions or whenever you want to promote school spirit.

Upgrade the printing. Use glossy paper for important materials. Add color when appropriate. Invest in a good clipart collection. Use outside printers for important projects. Upgrade the quality of your paper. Use a nice publishing program to sharpen up your presentations.

Classroom teaching devices. Parents love to see schools invest in things that benefit their students. Projection systems, computers, personal sound systems, internet access through the library, laser pointers, and video libraries are just the tip of the iceberg in the kind of things available for enhancing the classroom teacher's presentations.

DOUBLE-CHECK THE CONTENT

This may seem obvious, but it is essential that you ensure that all the information you want communicated is clearly stated. Make sure that you cover the basics:

- Who is involved?
- What is needed? (cost, materials, etc . . .)
- Where is it located?
- When will it occur?
- How do you arrive? (self, bus, etc . . .)
- When will it conclude?
- What is the purpose?

SOLICIT FEEDBACK

It is a good idea to occasionally get a read on how you are doing in terms of communicating to your students and their families. It is not always wise to send out evaluation forms, but the connected administrator has a network of individuals whom he or she can call and get an honest and frank evaluation as to how your communication is being received. Periodically, check in with folks and ask them for suggestions, areas for improvement, and things they would like to see repeated.

This one topic could require a whole book in and of itself before it is exhausted, but you should be able to begin here with some ideas for enhancing the quality and impact of your communication. But a change does not occur if someone does not take the initiative. That is *your* job. Stop right now and make a list of things you can do to make your area of communication more effective and start working on that list today. It will be a blessing to your students and to you as you get your message out and see it take root in the lives of those you serve.

Chapter Nine

Listening: It's More Than Just Sitting

"And so we dance the dance, each desperately trying to be heard, allowing ourselves to become the designated listener as long as the other promises to be our audience when it is our turn to step into the spotlight."

—Philip C. Johnson, Ph.D.

I was nervous. I was going to be interviewed on a local TV news show regarding a book I had co-authored. It was a live news-at-noon type show and I was running late for the interview. I was distracted to say the least. When I arrived at the studio I was rushed to a chair, fitted with an earpiece and quickly introduced to the anchor woman. The rest is pretty much a blur. I'm sure I must have answered her questions. I *tried* to look relaxed and knowledgeable. I probably did not succeed. When the show was over the anchor woman asked me if I would autograph a copy of my book for her. I said, "Sure, would you like me to make it out to Jennifer?" "Sure," she replied coolly, "If you want to, but *my* name is Deborah."

Oops . . . I hadn't been listening. I was so preoccupied with what I was going to say during the interview that I hadn't even bothered to pay attention to the name of my gracious TV hostess. Needless to say, to date I have not been invited back. (I was going to send a follow-up thank you note, but by the time I got back home I had forgotten her name . . . again.)

I love Nathan Miller's quote: "Conversation in the United States is a competitive exercise in which the first person to draw a breath is declared the listener." And so we dance the dance, each desperately trying to be heard, allowing ourselves to become the designated listener as long as the other promises to be our audience when it is our turn to step into the spotlight.

Listening is the forgotten half of communication. We easily focus on the active, participatory verbal portion of communication but fail to give attention to the seemingly passive aspect of the equation. Good listening is essential to developing and keeping relationships. Those who know how to listen well draw others to them. They become trusted confidants and their relationships take on a deeper hue. But true listening requires more than just sitting and staring at the speaker. At its foundation, listening requires an honest interest in what the other person is saying. Wise listeners also understand that when they fail to listen, they miss many clues to understanding others and how they view the world. Fortunately like many things, the skill of listening can be practiced and learned. Perhaps there's a reason God gave us two ears and only one mouth.

LISTENING ON PURPOSE

Christian educators spend much more time talking than listening. Teachers and administrators are in the business of disseminating information. Opportunities to practice listening come at stray moments before and after classes and during times of conferences and counseling. Educators are so used to having the answers and bestowing wisdom that taking the time to develop active listening skills is usually an afterthought. Yet it is often the ability to listen, to discern, and to understand that separates average communicators from great communicators.

When it comes right down to it, listening is a discipline of character. We can all choose to become better listeners when we begin to look at it as a choice and plan to listen with purpose. Consider some of these strategies to improve your listening skills:

Make a conscious choice to listen. Most people never intend to listen. Their focus is usually on themselves. Our goal is often to express thoughts and information for the sole purpose of feeling understood and validated. We spend more time worried about what our next response will be rather than honing in on what is being said to us.

Listening requires the right attitude. When listening, one needs to be open to the possibility that he just might learn something. The information that you hear may change you or enrich you in a surprising way. Listen with expectation.

Listening is not a "time out." Don't view listening as your turn to daydream or to rest or to plan your verbal comeback. Be active as you listen, offering non verbal affirmation as well as the appropriate grunts and "uh-huhs."

Listening requires time. Effective communication takes time and one needs to make time for it. You can't listen effectively if your mind is centered on your next appointment or your next activity. Also, don't be afraid to leave gaps. Silence allows for careful thought and measured responses.

Minimize potential distractions. Choose a quiet location for conversation. Don't expect to employ good listening techniques if you converse on the midway of the circus. Clowns and elephants do have the power to distract.

Facts vs. Emotions

When attempting to be a good listener, remember, you are not listening only for the purpose of gathering details. You are also listening for the emotions and feelings of the speaker. Failing to recognize the emotional element in any conversation will significantly limit your ability to listen effectively. The best listeners listen for what is said, what is not said, how things are phrased, as well as the indefinable emotional tenor of the dialogue.

Respond to feelings before facts. When someone is trying to communicate with you, information may be presented with an interesting mixture of fact and emotion. Often, the listener will be the most objective of the two people involved in the conversation. It is important to allow the speaker some measure of emotional freedom to express himself. The listener is wise to respond first to the emotional climate of the conversation before attempting to respond to the factual information that is being presented.

Often educators fail to recognize this important aspect of listening when they are involved in parent-teacher conferences or student counseling situations. Circumstances involving the well being of a parent's child will almost always prompt an emotionally charged conversation. Wise teachers and administrators will address the emotional issue first and then deal with the facts of the situation. To deal with the facts alone creates the impression that educators are not compassionate and much too objective.

Try to identify the flavor of what is being said. Beyond the mere words that are being shared, every conversation has a flavor. Sometimes the flavor provides more insight than the actual words. A careful listener will discern the tones of sarcasm, disappointment, revenge, bitterness, admiration, envy, or hope.

Don't mentally argue with the perspective of the speaker. Even if you promise yourself that you won't interrupt the speaker and openly disagree with him, there is still the temptation to disagree mentally. While the speaker is sharing, he may make a comment that you will struggle with. If you fly into a mental defense, you will miss part of the conversation and may lose the entire context of what was being communicated. Stay focused and open through the conversation withholding judgment until all has been said.

Don't jump to conclusions. Hear the person out before rushing to a conclusion. Most of us make up our minds about an issue by the fourth sentence. Once we've formed our conclusion we stop listening for information and sit silently in our own prejudice.

Listen with compassion. Compassion is not the same as condoning. Even when you do not agree with what is being shared, you can still offer compassion. A compassionate listening stance will also put the speaker at ease and allow them to speak more freely. The more information you gather, the better chance you'll have in guiding and helping the person later.

Understand before you solve. Sometimes our first instinct is to listen with the intent to solve the problems of others. While there are certainly times when solving is acceptable and desirable, there are other times when all the speaker really wants is a caring, sympathetic ear. People may already know all the "right" answers and may just need an opportunity to think out loud. The wise listener knows the difference between those who are seeking concrete advice and those who need an ear.

Responses That Encourage the Speaker

The verbal responses from the listener can either encourage or discourage the speaker from continuing. If your goal is to provide an understanding ear as well as to gain insight into your conversation partner, then it is in your best interest to provide responses that encourage the speaker to continue his conversation and keep him on track.

Paraphrase. Restating the information that has been shared with you helps the speaker to know that you've heard him and are on your way to understanding his efforts. This also provides an opportunity to clarify anything that may have been misunderstood.

Beware of sending out conversation stoppers. Have you ever started to share something with someone only to hear a comment from them that just made you want to clam up? Experienced listeners avoid comments that put a damper on the flow of expression. Common conversation stoppers include:

Interrupting. Interjecting too soon (or too often) sends the message that you aren't really "listening." Sit back and settle in for the long haul.

Finishing the other person's thoughts. I know . . . if people would talk faster and choose the correct words, we wouldn't have to do this. But it doesn't make it right. Good listeners are comfortable enough with their passive role to allow the speaker to dangle a bit and to struggle to find the right word. After all, the thoughts that need to be expressed are not yours.

Making light of the concerns of the speaker. Granted, different things are important to different people. But you can bet that if someone feels that their subject is important enough to share with you, then it's fairly important to them. If you treat the information too lightly or in any way diminish their concerns, you run the risk of offending and alienating the speaker.

Offering quick and trite answers. Life does not always come in neat packages. Clichés are best left in quote books.

Offering judgment or criticism. Try to remember if someone asked you for advice or if they asked you to listen. Even those who ask for advice don't often want it. Jumping in and offering criticism too early in the conversation will cause the speaker to shut down and cease sharing. There will be opportunities for redirecting thinking at the close of the conversation.

Patronizing. The polar opposite of being quick to judge or criticize is to patronize the speaker. In this case you utter words of agreement and understanding from the start to the finish of the conversation: "Uh-huh . . . ," "I see . . . ," "Of course . . . ," "You're absolutely right . . . ," "I know . . . ," "You are the best one in the office . . . ," and so on. Whether your motivation is to ingratiate yourself to the speaker or if you're just trying not to start trouble, this type of block will derail your conversation and preempt you from offering any future help to get this person back on track. Those who are attempting to share their hearts don't need to be jumped on and neither do they need to be agreed with excessively. They need an opportunity to share with someone who is actually interested in them.

Daydreaming. It's no fun to talk to someone who's not awake. I once worked with a man who always seemed to be thinking about something other than what I was talking about. His eyes would glass over and his stare would drift away from my eyes to some misty horizon. Then he'd get this silly little grin on his face that I am sure wasn't related to what I was saying. The give away was when I'd call his name and he'd jump and exclaim, "I'm listening!" Yeah, right. Then explain the drool on your chin and your ambient snoring.

Open yawning. I think we all know what this communicates. Stifle the temptation!

Ask open-ended questions. When attempting to respond to the speaker, do not use questions that can be answered with a simple "yes" or "no." This will not provide further insight into the other person. Ask questions that will provide you with more valuable information. Ask the speaker questions such as, "Why do you feel that way?", "Why do you believe that to be true?", or "How often do you find yourself in this situation?" This will prompt deeper thinking and more expressive communication.

Trying to discern the speaker's motives. Careful listening will reveal clues as to the motives of the speaker. Comprehending another's motives will allow you not only to address surface concerns, but deeper spiritual concerns as well. While listening, it's a good idea to mentally ask questions as the conversation progresses.

DE-PERSONALIZE YOUR LISTENING

Finally, if we want to become listeners that really hear others, we must de-personalize our listening habits. When we hear through the filters of our own biases, we're not really hearing others.

Avoid listening for what you want to hear. Occasionally while listening we conveniently filter out information that we're not comfortable with. We simply edit the speaker until we come up with a version of the conversation that we can live with. Effective listening requires honest listening. It is unwise and unhealthy to slip into denial over issues that you would rather not confront.

Avoid your biases. Everyone has biases. Before a conversation even begins most people have preconceived ideas about what will be said, how it will be said, and what they expect the end result will be. There is also a tendency to jump on one or two comments that prove our point or that we strongly identify with. Then we reconstruct the entire conversation to support our own personal bias.

Listen even when the topic is uncomfortably about *you*. No one wants to participate in a conversation where they turn out to be the villain. To have someone approach you and begin to share information that presents you in a less than flattering light is awkward to say the least. Our natural tendency is to immediately interrupt and attempt to refocus the negative attention elsewhere. But if listening is our goal it is important to apply the skill to conversations that involve us even when they highlight our worst qualities.

In order to accomplish this, you must remain open and honest regarding the information that is being shared. Choose to focus on what the speaker is sharing and try to understand it from their perspective. Avoid becoming defensive and attempt to address the issue at hand rather than throwing in statements and explanations designed to divert attention away from you. It is tempting to want to save face and try to explain and defend yourself, but it is important to realize that you do not always have to be right or totally understood by others. Once you have listened to the information that has been shared, respond in a biblically appropriate manner, ask for forgiveness if necessary and take appropriate steps to correct the situation.

Developing listening skills takes years of practice and, I believe, an entirely different set of muscles than those required to verbally express one's thoughts. Listening also has a completely different impact on others. If you thought that your witty sayings and insightful utterances could change the world, try the profundity of simply listening. As Voltaire said, "The road to the heart is the ear."

Chapter Ten

Dealing with Communication Breakdown: "I'm Communicating, but No One Seems to Be Paying Attention!"

"The first step in fixing a communication breakdown problem is to admit that there is one."

—Dan L. Burrell, Ed.D.

Virtually every administrator has gone through the process of having put an event on the annual school calendar and reminding the participants of the event through monthly updates or the school newsletter. In addition, you asked the teachers to remind the students in class and through assignment pad notations. Announcements were made over the school public address system and at the last PTF and it was even on the marquis in nine-inch high letters. Yet in the twenty-four hours preceding the scheduled event, your phones are jammed and your reception area is filled with parents who seem shocked that you would have planned such an important activity and then not give them enough warning. They have twenty questions, appear somewhat panicked, and more than a little frustrated. When you gently remind them that it was on this calendar and that announcement board, they look at you dumbly as if you were speaking in a foreign language consisting of clicks and whirring sounds.

Another classic case of communication breakdown is being played out. From the perspective of the administration, short of engraving it on the forehead of each and every child, they have adequately notified the parents of the activity. From the perspective of the "customers," you've kept them in the dark and set them up to look like bad parents who don't pay attention to what is going on in their child's life. Such scenarios are all too common in every organization and schools in particular. It is important for the administration of a Christian school to have a strategy for effectively communicating to the parents and avoiding breakdowns that will frustrate everyone involved.

Symptoms of Broken Communication

Broken communication emerges in multiple forms and it is important to be aware of it before a total collapse occurs. A few symptoms of broken communication would include:

Unreturned responses. If parents are not signing report cards, initialing assignment pads or returning work folders, chances are that the message isn't getting home.

Confusion regarding details. If the parents and students seem to be generally aware that there is something happening but have multiple questions regarding the time, location, cost, or other details of the event, it would appear that the communication may be inadequate or incomplete.

Frustrated feedback. When parents begin showing signs of confusion, irritation, or even anger over the child's progress, calendar items, or other routine items, this is a big signal that communication has been ineffective.

Complaints to the administration. Much communication is originated or initiated at the administrative level, but must be carried out at the faculty level. Be alert to pockets of feedback that come from a particular grade or class. Complaints regarding unreturned phone calls, inadequate notification of help classes, follow-up on notes written to the teacher, and other classroom-related issues should be a warning sign to the administration that a breakdown is occurring.

Poor participation. If people don't show up for events, money isn't turned in, papers aren't signed, or feedback isn't received, there obviously has been a breakdown somewhere. This is a loud indicator that something needs to be re-examined.

REPAIRING BROKEN COMMUNICATION

The first step in fixing a communication breakdown problem is to admit that there is one. Let's be honest, there are *many* occasions when we know we have done a good job of sending information home, and, for whatever reason, the message doesn't get through. So when we hear that parents are confused or frustrated, we in turn become frustrated. But the solution to frustration over mail service is not to shoot the postal patron, it is to find a more effective way to communicate.

The advertising industry has made a science of learning how to communicate to customers so they will buy the products of their clients. They test colors, size, key words (like "new" or "improved"), display location, and many other strategies in an effort to get their message across. Our generation is experiencing a plethora of communication options that make getting any single message to stand out among the others a difficult task. Just consider the different information topics you must address for the typical school year. There's school calendar, daily schedule, academic issues, classroom procedures, rules of conduct, financial policies, emergency policies, special events, regular events (chapel, end-of-quarter reviews, etc . . .) dress code, individual communication, athletic functions, fine arts events, field trips, class trips, competitions, report cards, school pictures, class dues, fund-raisers, church activities, special emphases, orientation procedures, and this list can go on *ad naseum*.

It really shouldn't come as a surprise that communication will sometimes conflict or struggle for attention. With all the potential for confusion, sometimes we mistakenly receive requests for more communication. Many times, the primary cause of communication breakdown is not too *little* communication, but too *much*! When a parent opens a book bag that is something akin to Fibber McGhee's closet and various calendars, notes, newsletters, and envelopes go flying in every which direction, chances are they will review none of it carefully and some of it not-at-all. That is why it is important to avoid communication overload.

Here are a few practical suggestions on how you might be able to condense and organize the various communication tools your school might utilize.

Put multiple announcements on a single communication instrument. Whether it is a weekly announcement sheet or a quarterly schedule of events, multiple communications from various departments will create a blizzard of paper that will bury the message you wish to transmit.

Do your homework in advance. Excessive and multiple communications is often the result of poor planning. Spur-of-the-moment announcements are another example that a preparation breakdown has occurred. Having a good grasp of the details well in advance of the scheduled event should enable the person doing the communication to put all the pertinent information down at the beginning. Communication that includes the phrase, "More details will be announced at a later date" screams that someone hasn't planned well or is doing things off the cuff.

Help the parents organize the information. Make sure the date of all information is included in a standard location. Color-coding communication is often helpful and can be accomplished in several ways. A different color of paper could be used for academics, athletics, and special events. Or you may want to have each month be represented by a color so that out-dated memos don't get piled up with current ones.

Have an administrator screen communication. Someone at an administrative level needs to be empowered with the responsibility to oversee and adjust communication. They should have the right to edit, revise, reschedule, or even pull communication that is ambiguous, redundant, or unnecessary.

Assign communication days. By assigning certain communication to specific days, you can train the parents to anticipate seeing some forms of communication. For example, you might want to send out announcement sheets every Friday. A folder of work for review could always be sent home on Monday. Report cards and mid-quarter progress reports could always go out on a Thursday. This way, the parent can be expecting some forms of communication by a regular calendar and look specifically for it.

Developing a Communication Strategy

Developing a strategy for getting pertinent information to your parents and families will always be a work in progress. You will find that adjustments will need to be made for grade levels, as technology advances, and whenever an existing method is no longer effective. For starters, let's examine methods of communicating to your parents.

Via students. For the brave (or slightly insane) educator, you may give information directly to a student to communicate to parents. It is very odd that the least effective form of communication is so widely-used, perhaps to provide an excuse for someone who was too lazy to try a more effective method of getting the news home.

Printed communication. Probably the most popular form, this method has increased with the advent of low-cost copying machines. The problem with this method is that it is easy, fast and everybody uses it. Therefore, much of your correspondence may be viewed as "junk mail" unless you figure out a way to grab their attention when they first see it.

Hand-written communication. A very effective form of sending a message home, but with large deficiencies. First, it is time consuming. Secondly, you will still be relying on a not-so-reliable delivery person in the form of the student in most cases. But the personal touch of communication should never be totally abandoned, particularly for an occasional note of praise or something that is personal and important.

Email communication. This is an exciting advancement in communication that may see much use in the future.

Well over fifty percent of your families probably have email accounts by now and they are available for little or no cost from many websites. Collect email addresses at the beginning of the year or on registration forms and make up a special folder in your address book for school correspondence. This can be done school-wide or on a class-by-class basis. By assigning each teacher an email account, you may also provide parents with quick and easy access to the teachers. Email can be answered when it is convenient or after hours. Email should be answered within twenty-four hours whenever possible. It is now possible to send photographs, files, and even audio clips via email.

Voice communication. Whether through a personal phone call or by leaving a message on a machine, it is often very effective to leave a personal voice message. Several excellent computer programs have been developed, which will allow your PC to call homes with a pre-recorded message during certain hours. Also, you may be wise to leave messages during the day, during your break period, or right after school on home answering machines for general items. Make sure that you don't drop bad news on them via a recording however. Finding out that you will be retaining Johnny in third grade should not be done via an answering machine.

Published communication. This is different from printed communication in that it is published as part of a school-wide information blitz. For example, it is a good idea to publish the school calendar in several locations such as the student handbook, school-supplied book jackets, assignment pad covers, etc. You may also have a month or quarterly school newspaper that can have a section for parent information.

Centralized bulletin boards. For school-wide correspondence, it is sometimes a good idea to keep a bulletin board in a central area where parents frequent and put the latest memos on it.

Website communication. This is a burgeoning method for communication with unlimited applications. Keep your school calendar posted, have a "special notice" section, put lists of students who have received recognition (e.g., honor roll, students of the week, etc.), or have a page for each class. Some schools are even posting homework assignments and test dates for individual classes on their sites. When students miss school because of illness, parents are encouraged to download the assignments from the school website. This is a growth area for communication and needs to be seriously considered by your school.

Of course, there are other methods of communication, but you will find that those already listed are either the most frequently used and/or the most effective.

A Strategy for Getting Your News Home

Begin by educating your parents. This may be the single most important thing that you will do in improving communication. Educating is a nice word for "train." In as much as the success of your classroom control and progress is often established the first few weeks of the school year for the students, the success of your communication is often dependent upon how you train the parents regarding communication. Tell them exactly how you will be communicating to them, what you will communicate, how they may communicate to you, when communication will be sent home, etc.

Refer back to your communication system frequently. When a parent does not read something that was sent home or hasn't followed the procedure, point out to them that they have already received the information in a gentle, but clear way. "Mrs. Brown, yes, there is a field trip tomorrow for Susan's class and they do need to bring a lunch. You might want to check last week's assignment sheet where it is written in Thursday's square. Also, it has been on our class website page since the beginning of the year." You don't need to be condescending, but you do need to help your parents to watch for the communication you work hard to produce.

Have annual communication. This would include a yearly update of the parent/student manual and the school calendar. You might also want to make sure that the orientation, financial, and uniform (if you use uniforms) procedures are clearly published.

Have quarterly communication. This should be a reminder of items coming up in the next nine weeks. Any adjustments (which should be few) should be noted on the quarterly updates. This should be sent directly to the home through the mail.

Have monthly communication. This calendar should be something that can be placed on the front of your refrigerator. It might include days out of school, special programs, and the lunch menu for the month. It will generally be posted on the refrigerator of most school families and referred to often.

Have weekly communication. This would be from individual teachers. Classroom teachers should be responsible for keeping their parents informed. A weekly handout that parents know to look for each Friday might include next week's homework assignments, tests or announced quiz dates, special instructions, and fun information like birthdays or class announcements. Again, these will most likely be kept on the front of a refrigerator.

Develop a school website. This is no longer optional. If you haven't developed a school website, you will not attract sophisticated school families, and you will lose many opportunities. It does not have to be elaborate or expensive. However you should begin the development of a website immediately if you have not done so already. Also, it is extremely important that you keep the website updated frequently. Refer to it in all of your literature and find a URL which is easy to remember. Even if you are using a rented server for your website, you can have your own domain name.

Be patient. It is easy to get frustrated with parents who don't pay attention. But sometimes we just need to settle down and remember that this is a part of human nature. You don't need the stress of fretting excessively over parents who don't pay attention or students who don't get word home. Just smile and patiently explain (for the ten thousandth time) what is needed, remind them how to find the information the next time, and then send them on their way. It's not worth the raised blood pressure and the anxiety to grow angry when communication breaks down.

You should always be checking to see how communication is flowing in your school. Make sure that you are communicating positive things and not just calendar information or negative news. Parents love to get positive notes, encouraging emails, a quick voice mail of praise or a thumbs up across the parking lot. When you sense that communication isn't all that it should be, find the problem and develop a strategy for repair. Everyone will appreciate your efforts!

Chapter Eleven

Awkward Communication: Dealing with Difficult Topics

"Showing compassion and sympathy ought to be the forte of the Christian communicator. It should be a hallmark of the redeemed."
—Philip C. Johnson, Ph.D.

CAN WE TALK ABOUT SOMETHING ELSE?

When I was much younger, (hopefully telling you right up front that I was younger will provide me some limited excuse for the social ineptitude I reveal in the following story) a friend of mine lost her first baby. It was such a sad situation. She and her husband were so looking forward to the birth of this child. My heart grieved for their loss, but for some reason I just couldn't think of anything that I felt was appropriate enough to say. So I just avoided saying anything. Circumstances were such that I didn't see the couple on a daily basis and time went by—too much time—an embarrassing amount of time. Still I hadn't said anything. The more time that passed, the more awkward it became. Finally, feeling like such an idiot, I called and apologized for my stupidity and offered my sympathies and shared a little in their grief. It was amazing that I had agonized so extensively over what I would or could say to this couple when they simply wanted to know that I cared and that I hurt for them.

Educators will be faced with numerous situations that will be undeniably difficult to address. Students fail courses. Teachers don't always get the promotions they want. School families suffer tragedies. People make poor decisions. Sometimes we shy away from communication because these topics are painful. Other times we simply don't know what would be appropriate. When people are experiencing hurt or disappointed, it doesn't fit in with our concept that all of life should be wrapped up with a tidy little ending like a thirty-minute sitcom. As a result we shy away from the challenge of addressing the uncomfortable topic.

Communicating Bad News

Not too many people look forward to communicating bad news to others. (Granted, there are a few who are gifted in this area, like the IRS and my third grade teacher who had an odd affection for her red pen and marking incorrect answers on my paper; but we'll deal with them later in another therapy session.) Can you imagine if your boss fired you but never told you the bad news? You'd just keep coming in to work, and maybe over time, you'd realize that someone else was doing your exact job and that you were no longer getting paid for your services. Perhaps it would eventually dawn on you that you'd been terminated. Bad news is not pretty, but even ugly information must be communicated. Not knowing the bad news or pretending that it does not exist does not make the bad news go away.

Bad news can come in a plethora of forms and can elicit a variety of responses from those who are the recipients.

From the student receiving his first "B" on a report card, to the girl who finds out her boyfriend likes someone better, to losing a job or losing a loved one, bad news needs to be handled with care and precision appropriate for the occasion. When you need to share unpleasant information, consider the following strategies:

Don't drop bad news suddenly. Some people are more fragile than others and the sudden shock of unpleasant information may cause increased distress. Rather, you should gently prepare the individual for the forthcoming information. If the situation allows it, keep the individual closely informed on the progression of their particular circumstances. If a student is going to fail a course or if a teacher is not going to have a contract renewed, it should never come as a complete surprise.

Share bad news with compassion. Bad news is bound to come with emotional reactions. Sometimes, in order to maintain some measure of control over our own emotions, we deliver the information with cold detachment. But superior communicators always consider the emotions of others. You don't have to burst into tears or wear sackcloth and ashes to communicate a little compassion, but you can show genuine concern.

Deliver disturbing news in person. Are you more comfortable faxing or emailing bad news? Why not just wait and let them read about it in the newspaper or in the announcement section of the church bulletin? It is the coward that does not have the strength to face someone with bad news. The personal touch may not make the bad news any better, but it does communicate a basic respect for the dignity of the other.

Attempt to frame the news with perspective. Some news is just too horrific to place into any immediate context. Losing a child or hearing that your wife has just been diagnosed with cancer, require time, processing and supernatural grace from God in order to cope. Lesser tragedies, including the loss of a boyfriend, the loss of a job or the emergence of an inopportune pimple can benefit from a little perspective setting.

Offering Sympathy

"I'm sorry . . ." "I know just how you feel . . ." "You don't deserve this . . ." They all sound sort of trite don't they? Welcome to the old war horses of sympathy phraseology. If someone suffers a loss or a disappointment, we just pull out a stock phrase and sling it in the hurting party's general direction. Having completed our duty, we return to our regular lives allowing others to pull their own pieces together.

Throughout their ministry careers, educators will have opportunities to offer sympathy to a variety of people, including students, school parents, coworkers and of course their own family, friends, and neighbors. Showing compassion and sympathy ought to be the forte of the Christian communicator. It should be a hallmark of the redeemed. But like many things, the art of offering appropriate empathy has become lost amidst the stale and mundane responses that are all too often offered. To enhance the impact of your sympathy, consider these thoughts:

Offer a simple but sincere, "I'm sorry." Often no more and no less than this simple phrase will do. After agonizing over all of the possibilities and trying to find something appropriate and sincere, you will find that a simple expression of sorrow on behalf of someone else will communicate exactly what you want.

Mention people by name. When someone loses someone they love we are not always sure what we should say. Should you mention the person by name or will doing so simply bring back sad memories? In reality, everyone is aware that the departed person is no longer with us. Just because you choose not to mention the person by name doesn't mean that the bereft will forget their loss. Go ahead and refer to the person by name and let others know how much you miss their presence. It shows respect and honor for memories and for those who are suffering the loss.

Share a touching anecdote about the person concerned. People die, they go off to college, and they move too far away. A person's life and the time they've shared with you should be celebrated. Why not share a great story or a wonderful memory about the person who has touched your life. It will warm the hearts of all those who miss that person's presence.

Offer specific concrete help. When attempting to offer help to someone as a sign of sympathy, avoid the nebulous offer of, "Call me if you need anything!" Most people will not take advantage of such a weak offer. Instead, offer concrete help such as, "I'll be by tomorrow with a meal." "I'll make sure that your grass is cut this weekend." "Let me take the kids for a couple of days while you take care of other things."

Send flowers or gifts. Flowers and gifts also provide an opportunity to show kindness and sympathy towards others. Sending these things not only provides an opportunity to express your kind wishes but they offer a lingering reminder of your thoughtfulness.

Do not over dramatize. There is no need to over identify with the hurting person. The situation is probably difficult enough without heightening the drama with statements such as, "This is the worst tragedy I've ever seen!" and "I have never seen anyone treated so abominably in my life!" There's no need to stoke the emotional fires.

Don't say, "I know exactly how you feel." As much as we might want to connect with the hurting or disappointed party, the afore mentioned phrase is never appropriate. The truth is, you don't know *exactly* how anyone feels and to say so implies either arrogance or it trivializes the individual's grief.

Don't offer advice. During any tragedy emotions are high. This means that it is not an ideal time for you to offer advice. If you say, "Well, if I were you I'd just up and quit!" That person just might do that. If someone loses their husband of forty-five years and you say, "You know, you ought to move to Phoenix and start over," they might just follow that suggestion. Of course that suggestion may have sounded good during an emotional period, but it doesn't take in to consideration that doing so will separate that person from forty-five years of friends, a church, and other good memories. Allow people to wade through the emotional waters before suggesting significant changes.

Avoid clichés.
- "Chin up." (What does that mean anyway? It sounds more like a callisthenic.)
- "You'll get over it." (Some people never do.)
- "Time heals all wounds." (You're just begging someone to smack you.)
- "Don't cry." (I will if I want to . . . don't tell me what to do.)

- "They were too young to die." (Aren't we all?)
- "He's in a better place now." (I know that, but I'd much rather have them with me now!)
- "At least they're out of their misery." (Yes, but I'm just beginning mine.)
- "I feel almost worse about this than you do." (You could not possibly feel worse about this than I do. How dare you!)
- "Life goes on." (Oh, but at the moment, I wish it wouldn't.)

How to Say "No"

Another fascinatingly difficult word to utter is the word "no." In the greater Communication Empire, it is a rather small word, but apparently has become a very difficult word to pronounce. (Again, there are exceptions to this. My mother never seemed to have trouble saying this word to me.) There are times when it is not only acceptable to say "no," but better to say it. Sometimes you will have no other choice but to say "no" to others: "No, you did not get the job" or "No, I'm not going to approve your project" or "No, I will not round off your C+ to an A-," or "No, I will not buy your cookies little girl, now go away." When learning how to use the word "no" consider these thoughts:

The honesty angle. Be honest with yourself. Be honest about what you can and cannot do. Everyone has limited time and resources. Also choose to be honest with others. You will not be able to do everything for everyone. It is impossible to please every person. Be straightforward with people regarding your answers. Don't hedge and make others think that you'll provide some service when you really have no intention of doing so. Respect people enough to tell them the truth. If you don't have the time, ability or desire to grant someone's request, then simply tell them so.

Saying "no" without the guilt. Many of the things we may end up saying "no" to, are not necessarily bad things. There are lots of good people, projects and requests that we will not be able to participate in. The problem is the false guilt that often accompanies the pronunciation of the word "no." This very same guilt is the reason that many of us are over-extended and frustrated in our lives and ministries.

The word "no" does not have to come wrapped in a layer of guilt. If you've been truthful, thoughtful, and kind in your responses, you must not allow others to manipulate you and your emotions. If you have been asked to do something and you are feeling rushed and pressured, ask for time to think before providing your final answer. Clarify in your own mind what you are actually capable of doing and doing well. Then embrace your decision and choose not to feel obligated to another. After all, you know yourself better than anyone else and you also know what your current commitments are. The person who begs and pleads with you to meet their expectations is often just trying to make his own life easier. He is not always thinking about your best interests. This is not to say that we don't give sacrificially of ourselves to others, but we need to invest our lives with wisdom and with an understanding of stewardship.

A variety of ways to say "no." There are many ways to utter your negative response. Predictably, some are geared toward being more gracious than others:

The uncaring "no." This "no" resonates with disregard for others and their feelings. It can convey more than just an answer to a question. It may also express a negative value toward the idea and the person requesting it.

The passive "no." This is a "no" hidden behind an excuse. It lacks honesty and integrity.

"No" disguised as a "yes." This response seems very agreeable on the surface but there is no follow through. What sounded like a "yes" in the verbal sense turns out to be a "no" in the physical sense. This response sends confusion and presents you as a coward.

The "maybe-later" no. Sometimes we have to say "no" to a request that we would, at a different time, have said "yes" to. Because it is simply a matter of timing, your refusal can be expressed with a request to ask you again at another time.

The "no" with an alternative. If you cannot or will not be able to provide something for someone, you can always say "no" and then provide the person with a possible alternative. *"No, I won't be able to give you a ride to the airport, but I believe that Tim is heading in that direction. Why don't you ask him?"*

The firm-but-kind "no." Many people feel that there are two ways to say "no." There is the weak, apologetic "no" or the "I'm-fed-up-with-all-these-requests-and-now-I'm-angry-no." The proper alternative is a "no" said with firmness as well as kindness. There is no need to make excuses or to explain all your reasons. The "no" should be enough. Being clear and firm does not preempt our ability to be gracious.

Offering Criticism

Isn't it interesting how we "offer" criticism to others like we were offering them a piece of candy? And on some level we sort of expect them to be eager to accept our "gift" of criticism. Let's face it, unless you've got a nasty streak or are insanely egotistical, criticizing others can be difficult. Yet there are times when it will become necessary to share criticisms. Keep these things in mind when attempting to tread this awkward terrain:

Double-check your motives before criticizing others. If we are not really careful, we run the risk of falling into the habit of fault-finding for the purpose of making ourselves look better or for the purpose of advancing our own agendas. Make sure that criticisms are always objective and that your heart is right before God. (Psalm 139:23)

Be sensitive to personal-criticism choices. Serving up criticism is like serving steaks. Some like it well done while others like it medium rare. Still others like it "tartar." In the same way, if people must accept criticism, some would rather have you come and offer it in person while others would prefer it to be in written form. Some want it straight while others want it sugarcoated. Be sensitive to the individual.

Don't drop the dreaded note. Students, employees and friends are not waiting around hoping for their weekly shot of criticism. When it becomes necessary to share criticism be sensitive to how you initiate the meeting. Don't drop a note in someone's faculty or student mailbox with the cryptic, "I need to see you." or "We need to talk." Doing so sends some into a panic until the dreaded meeting time finally arrives. If you can, avoid the note altogether and initiate the meeting when you have the time to discuss the issue. If you do need to leave a note, reference the nature of the meeting, "I need to see you about your new raise!" or "I need to see you regarding your student, Carl." At least they'll know what to worry about all day.

Make sure you have all the facts first. Your choice to offer a word of criticism needs to come only after you have carefully gathered all of the facts. Wrongly criticizing others will significantly damage your relationship giving others the impression that you don't trust them and won't give them the benefit of the doubt. Check the facts before you pounce.

Use criticism sparingly. The impact will be much greater if those around you don't hear you criticize very often.

Never criticize others publicly. Most people have a low tolerance for public humiliation. Being called down in public can be devastating. Whether criticizing a student, teacher or co-worker, do it privately.

Focus on behavior first and motives second. This is particularly difficult to do. I have always linked values and motives to behavior. Scripture links the two together as well. (Proverbs 4:23) But I have found that when you dig too deeply into the motives of others—the "why" behind the actions—it often prompts defensive and angry behavior. In light of that, it is sometimes wiser to deal with the behavior and trust the Holy Spirit to deal with the heart. This does not mean that you do not employ discernment in dealing with people; it simply means that your goal is not necessarily to get them to admit the motive behind the behavior, but to change the behavior.

Be specific in your criticism. If you're going to go to the trouble of letting someone know that you're unhappy with him, at least provide enough information so that he knows what needs to be improved. A friend of mine had heard through the grapevine and then finally from his supervisors that his job performance was not up to par. And yet, when talking to his employer, he could never pin down exactly what behaviors and skills were the problem. He lost his job, but it left him frustrated and unable to address any particular weakness.

Don't give multiple criticisms. Sometimes we save up our criticisms and then we have some sort of "going out of criticism" sale. When approaching someone with a concern, voice only one concern at a time. Don't save them up and let them all gush out at once. That may be more than one individual can bear.

Be constructive. Don't just allow a criticism to lie there. Let the student, friend, employee, or coworker hear some suggestions for correcting the problem.

Handling Criticism

If offering criticism can be awkward, accepting criticism can be excruciating. Our natural reflexes cause us to lash out at those who would dare criticize us. We can easily become defensive and verbally abusive to our perceived attacker. Most of us, however sterling our character may be, are not likely to escape the critical observations of others. Folks, if they look hard enough (and believe me, they will!) they will find something to disparage.

Consider the Source. Sometimes criticism is unwarranted. People do have their own agendas and reasons for trying to accuse and discourage. From time to time the character of the source of the criticism discounts the information.

Look at the criticism honestly. Not all criticism needs to be discounted. The wise person, who is truly interested in personal growth, will take an honest look at any criticism. He will identify and address the weakness in a truthful fashion.

Don't ask for criticism. Sometimes we invite criticism by simply not doing what we are supposed to be doing. If you choose not to follow through on your commitments and responsibilities you are inviting others to criticize you and you should not be surprised.

Don't become defensive. Just relax and listen. Whether you agree with what is being said or not, at least you need to listen. Becoming defensive makes you look guiltier anyway.

Don't attack. Yes, it is tempting to lash out at those who would cause us pain. But the very person who is sharing the unpleasant information with you may have your best interest at heart. Listen to them.

Don't pretend that it doesn't bother you. Of course criticism bothers us! If we pretend we don't care, we expend a lot of needless energy. Expect that criticism is going to bother you.

Don't overreact. At the same time that we admit criticism is bothersome, we don't need to go to the other extreme and overreact. Keep things in perspective.

Don't kick the "dog." If your administrator tells you that you need to shape up in certain areas, don't go back to the classroom and take it out on your students.

Express apologies or regrets. After you've heard and considered the words of criticism, express your sincere apologies and do what you can to make amends.

Get on with life. Put it behind you. What's done is done, what's said is said. Take what value you can from the information shared with you, grow from it, and determine to move beyond it.

Chapter Twelve

What's Your Claim to Fame? Communicating Your School's Identity

"Your school projects an image to the community and that can actually be one of your greatest or most detrimental communication tools."
—Dan L. Burrell, Ed.D.

It is no surprise that institutions develop reputations within their communities. Within the community where I live, there are many Christian schools. When I hear the name of each of those schools, an instant impression of that school crosses my mind. There's the Christian preparatory school for rich kids, there's the small church-member-only school where they wear uniforms, there's the Christian-in-name-only school that has a rather poor reputation, there's the learn-at-your-own pace school, there's the school nestled on a beautiful park-like campus, there's the school with the outstanding computer education program, and there's the school with the sports teams that always seem to be in the newspapers. Each of these schools, for better or for worse and on purpose or not, has a certain claim to fame within our community.

If someone were to describe your school, what characteristics or qualities would they use to describe your program, student body, facilities or faculty? Would those adjectives be positive or negative? Are they the same words you would choose to describe your school or have they been chosen for you?

Part of effective communication is the responsibility of a proactive administrator. Your school projects an image to the community and that can actually be one of your greatest or most detrimental communication tools. It can be a stigma or it can be an asset. But either way, it is the responsibility of the leadership to identify and mold how the community, your constituents, and even your own team views and perceives your over-all ministry.

The first step in communicating a positive message to your community is to know who you are. Many schools make the mistake of trying to be "all things to all people." Even public schools with their large coffers of resources are no longer trying to do that. With magnet programs, focused curricula and specialized agendas, they work to distinguish their schools, or at least divisions of it, as outstanding from the others in some particular way.

Christian schools, with their much more limited resources, doubly need to define why they exist, whom they are serving, and what they are trying to accomplish. There is no single or best answer for every school. Some Christian schools have wide-open enrollment policies while others restrict theirs to church members only or those who have a certain IQ. Some exist as an alternative to public schools, some are boarding schools to help troubled kids or perhaps missionary parents, others still are specialized for those who are handicapped or have special needs. Some are trying to produce an academically superior graduate, some are desiring their grads to be spiritual above all else and others are producing "experts" in a particular field such as technology or fine arts.

For several years, the business community has kept the development of a mission statement in vogue. Many companies have spent thousands of hours and dollars trying to develop a single, one-sentence statement that summarizes their "mission"—their reason for doing business. I've seen the process of developing a mission statement become so complex and convoluted that I think it did more damage to the institution than it did good. On the other hand, I've also seen churches, schools and businesses develop a concise and clearly-worded statement which not only clarifies why they exist in the mind of their leadership and employees, but which becomes their claim to fame within their community.

Here are some questions you might want to consider as you develop a statement of who you are.
- Whom do we serve?
- Why do we exist?
- What are we trying to produce?
- How do we produce it?
- What are other dynamics that should be addressed (spiritual, physical, family, etc.)?
- How will we be measured or evaluated?

Knowing who you are and why you exist is obviously just the first step to communicating your school's identity clearly and accurately to the community you serve and in which you do business.

Showing Your Best Side

Everyday, we make decisions as to what we will reveal to others about ourselves. Thankfully, we often have choices in that matter. We decide how we dress, our personal grooming, what our topics of conversation will be, and with whom we will interact. In general, we almost always try to show our best side.

Every school has problems. Poor facilities, underpaid teachers, ornery students, limited financial resources, and underdeveloped programs are realities in many schools. But we can't let them define us to our community. No school is perfect. But for every liability, we have corresponding assets.

Compassionate and caring teachers, reasonable tuition, Christian curricula, biblical discipline, traditional philosophy and, connected families are just a few that may be found in your school. It is the responsibility of the leadership of the school to make sure that the best side is emphasized and on display.

In as much as showing your best side personally is the result of initiative and attention on your part as you shower each morning, deal with unruly hair, pick out appropriate attire, and arrange your personal schedule, you will also only project the best side of your school through a series of careful and conscious choices, initiative and attention.

Ways in Which You Project Your School's Identity

There are many ways you will be projecting an image to your community. Some of these give you opportunity to manipulate (Note: The word "manipulate" does not always have to carry a negative connotation. In this sense, it involves a proactive usage of strengths and opportunities to do something positive for your school.) your strengths, uniqueness, and distinguishing characteristics in order to project a positive and inviting image. Here are a few ways you will project your school's identity:

Campus Appearance. Do you have a clean and orderly campus? Check your buildings for maintenance items. Try to look at your campus and facilities as if this was your first time to see them. It is amazing how we grow accustomed to campus blemishes because we see them every day. Is there helpful signage to direct guests? Make sure that details such as landscaping, paint, safety issues, parking and security are up-to-date.

Student Appearance. Every child in your school is a walking, talking billboard. This fact is another argument for student uniforms, in my opinion. Are your students attired and groomed in such a way that they are distinctively identified with Christ or would you draw another conclusion? Does your dress code promote order and a serious attitude toward their education? Do the students look like sharp, disciplined ambassadors of the Lord and your ministry?

Homebound Communication. Nothing screams a negative message louder than a tacky, poorly constructed, and grammatically weak letter to parents. If the letters from the administration and faculty don't pass an excellence muster, how can we expect to produce excellence in our students? Make sure that your correspondence has been proof-read, that the mechanics and lay-out of the letter is appropriate, and that you use decent quality paper, ink, and envelopes. Another area of attention is report cards. Most schools have gone to computer generated report cards and they generally look sharp. Make sure names are correct and addresses are updated.

Facility Maintenance. From the condition of the playground to the lighting in the classroom, daily, weekly and monthly inspections should be performed to make sure that equipment, furnishings and facilities are pleasing to the eye and safe for the students. Burned-out light bulbs, dirty windows, chipped paint, broken desks, items stored in plain view, decaying carpeting, inadequately stocked restrooms, broken playground equipment, cluttered cabinets and walls, stained ceiling tiles, and many other detail issues can leave a negative impression to the campus guest or parent. Many schools approach furnishing their classrooms with a "swap-shop" mentality that mixes and matches desks, chairs, cabinets and storage units from a variety of sources. Develop a uniform furnishings strategy to give your school a warm, but professional appearance. Don't encourage the teachers to bring the old cabinets leftover from their latest kitchen remodeling to the classroom.

Programs and Activities. It is better to have one outstanding student production or program each year than three that are poorly-planned and executed. Spend extra time on costumes, memorization, projection, transitions, and special touches that will wow the parents with the excellence of your presentation. Make sure you have good open-house events scheduled throughout the year to display or demonstrate your student's work and progress. On PTF nights, coordinate your schedules to allow for the science fair displays to be in the cafeteria or use regional or state fine arts contestants to provide the program. Consider using video or slide presentations as a prelude to the program or as a part of the PTF itself.

Media relations. I will say more about this later on, but many local and neighborhood publications would love to list your calendar of events or provide a photographer to catch a few pictures of some special activity for their publication. Assign one person to compile a list of fax numbers or email addresses for all the area media outlets and fax or email them a list of events with the who, where, when, and how of each item. You'll be surprised at how many of them show up in print or on the air. You want the community to be hearing the name of your school very frequently.

Use creative advertising. Among the least effective forms of advertising is simply buying a newspaper ad. The smart dollars are spent elsewhere. Use school bumper stickers to recognize outstanding students like students of the month or honor roll students. Parents will almost always put them on their car to advertise the fact that they have given birth to superior progeny. Have students purchase t-shirts for special activities at a reduced price and make sure that the name of your school is prominently displayed. The child who walks through the mall wearing a Community Christian School Field Day shirt is a billboard in tennis shoes. Other ideas include refrigerator magnet calendars, school license plates, school folders, optional school hats or book bags, and even school jackets. Park your buses near the street. Keep a changeable school marquis in a highly visible area. Have your choirs sing in churches or at the mall around Christmas time.

Watch image issues. Several areas can become negative public relations issues that communicate messages that you want to avoid. Be careful about how often you ask for funds in addition to your tuition. Having a dozen fund-raisers, adding fees constantly, asking for donations becomes wearisome. Charge reasonable tuition, limit special fund-raisers to no more than two per year and consolidate the weekly or occasional fees to one annual activity fee and you won't appear to be reaching in to parent's pockets constantly. Have your staff dress professionally while they are on campus. Don't allow after-school staff to sit in the shade while the children are wrestling in the mulch as the parents come on and off your campus. Make sure kids aren't roaming, unsupervised across the campus. Have teachers and safety patrols in position during drop-off and pick-up. Make sure visitors to campus are screened and have identification tags on. Use sign-out sheets when parents pick up students. Check the identification of anyone picking up a student. These are all seemingly small, but very significant image issues that have the power of communicating something very positive or somewhat negative about your school.

Courteous Interaction. A satisfied customer will tell a few people; a dissatisfied customer will tell a few hundred people. Make sure that your staff returns phone calls promptly, answers letters in a timely way, and follows through on commitments. Spend extra time training the accounts receivable clerks on how to handle financial matters discreetly and positively. Make sure the person who answers the phone does so cheerfully and courteously. Have the sharpest, friendliest person possible be in the position of first interaction with the parents when they visit the office. Encourage teachers to send positive notes home or to leave positive voice messages. Proactive and positive communication from the school will create good-will and limit frustration.

Making the Media Your Friend

Your relationship with the local media is like tending to a garden. It requires on-going investment, careful nurturing and a watchful eye. Remember that most reporters are very busy people who are always under a deadline and who have an editor breathing down their neck. They need eye-catching and interesting information. If they appear to be biased, they are probably unaware of it. They are in a competitive industry, so they are often aggressive.

Many Christians make a mistake by viewing all members of the media from a negative perspective. Make no mistake, there are many people in the media who are no friend to conservative Christian organizations. But there are more who are either ignorant of the movement, misinformed, or who really don't have a strong opinion one way or another. When you approach a reporter or editor with immediate hostility, you may cause them to question why you are behaving in such a way and surmise that you must be afraid of or hiding something. Following are some practical ideas for working with the media in your community.

Meet and cultivate a relationship with the specific reporters that cover your area. This might include education, religion, values, sports, local, and family reporters and editors. When they call for a comment or with a question, get back to them quickly. They have a job to do also.

Alert them to items that might interest them. If you are having a big-name speaker in for a fund-raising banquet, try to arrange a private interview. If you are building the world's largest ice cream sundae, let them know about it. Invite them for positive events that provide a human or community interest angle for an article or photograph.

Drop them positive feedback from time to time. Usually, much of the feedback a report receives is critical. When you see them write something positive, call or write them with a short comment of appreciation or encouragement. Reporters are people, too and they like to know they make a difference.

Have one person be the point person for the ministry. They should be the contact person for event-driven announcements. Have them handle media correspondence and the issuance of press releases.

Be aware of the rules. When speaking to a reporter, always make sure you are aware of whether or not you are "on the record." You always have the right to make conversation "off the record" which means you won't be quoted, and your words will not to be cited in an article. Reporters often use this as a way of getting background for a story. You may also ask to be off the record so that you can educate the reporter without seeing your name and an edited version of your comments in the morning paper. *Always remember*, you are accountable for your words, and you need to be very careful that they are thoughtful, accurate, and reasonable. Don't forget that any portion of a sentence or comment may be the only portion of what you say to make it in print or on the air regardless of its context. Never forget that you are talking to a reporter and that if they are doing their job, they are looking for news and comments. By the way, by developing a relationship with a reporter, you may request a "heads-up" on articles of interest that might affect you, an opportunity to give back-ground or perspective, and professional consideration before a story is aired or published. If you have a tendency to speak flippantly, to get extremely nervous during an interview, or to have difficulty communicating in a balanced and coherent way, then leave the press communication to someone else. Some people are comfortable with it and others aren't. Don't try to force it if you weren't born to work in this arena.

Develop a strategy for negative press coverage. On occasion, something will happen in your school that will create a controversy. You'd better have a strategy for dealing with the firestorm that may be created. I've seen schools turn small disasters into total public relationship nightmares, because they didn't know how to handle a negative press situation. In my years as an educator, I've seen schools deal with items from tragic student deaths, immorality from a classroom teacher, hurricane damage, booming enrollment, dropping enrollment, plane crashes, bus wrecks, student lawsuits, child abuse, student threats, and myriad other situations that had the potential to be "explosive" if mishandled with the media. In some cases, it was handled wisely and in other cases, it was a mess. The following suggestions will help you deal with negative press coverage.

Have a single spokesman for the entire ministry. Demand that no employees speak with any member of the press except for the approved spokesman. All reporters should be referred to that person. Multiple messengers provide the opportunity for confusion and controversy. Don't allow students to give interviews during negative situations while on campus. Ask parents and students to refer reporters to the administration and request that they not give interviews. You can't require this, but it doesn't hurt to ask.

Rely on written press releases. Many times, it is best to issue a press release simultaneously to all media outlets with the official response of the school.

When necessary, seek legal counsel. In our litigious society, we need to be very careful about what, if any, comments are appropriate to make. If a controversy erupts over a student dismissal, you may open yourself to a potential lawsuit by commenting on the case publicly.

Stick to your points. Don't necessarily answer every question that is put to you with a response to the question. Transition to the point you want to make. An exchange may go like this: Reporter: "Principal Jones, explain to us how little Bobby Smith received a concussion on your playground from a piece of equipment that was over twenty years old."

Principal Jones: "We are still investigating the incident with our student, and I'm not prepared to comment on that investigation while it is on-going. However, I can tell you that we inspect all of our equipment on a monthly basis and have just recently renovated our playground with the proceeds of a school-wide fund-raiser. Over seven hundred children attend our school each day, and this is the first incident in many months of a serious injury. We recognize that children have accidents and that no safety procedure is fail-safe, but we have an on-going commitment to the protection and safety of all of our students and our record confirms that." You never really answered the question, but you did get to state several important realities that need to be heard by the audience.

Remember, you don't have to say anything. Sometimes "no comment" is the best response. You can always delay your answer until a more appropriate time.

Make sure you have emotional control. It is unwise to get angry, weep, appear breathless or agitated, or in any way give the impression of anything less than confidence, self-control, and leadership.

Communicate to your parents first. Don't make them find out details second hand. Honest, early, and up-front information will be appreciated by them and will reassure them that you are on top of the situation and will communicate directly to them. People often jump to negative conclusions in the midst of an information vacuum.

Communicating your school's identity is something that needs to be carefully considered. You will need to groom and nurture that identity. It will require maintenance, assignment of resources, and regular attention. But it can also become an inexpensive form of advertising and promotion as you demonstrate excellence, professionalism, Christ-likeness, and initiative.

To order additional copies of

PERSPECTIVES IN CHRISTIAN EDUCATION

Have your credit card ready and call

(877) 421-READ (7323)

or send $10.95 each + $3.95* S&H to

WinePress Publishing
PO Box 428
Enumclaw, WA 98022

*add $1.00 S&H for each additional book ordered

If you are interested in scheduling seminars, lectures or if you are interested in information on their other ministries, Dr. Johnson can be reached at: DrPCJ@aol.com and Dr. Burrell can be reached at DBurrell@northsidebapt.org.